DRESSING UP

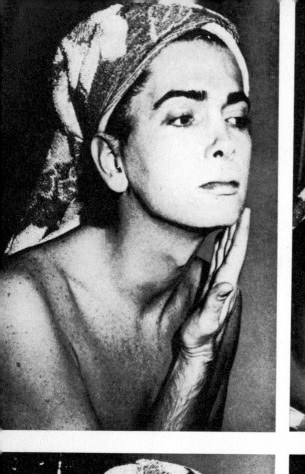
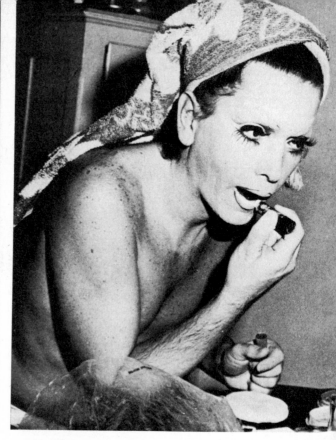
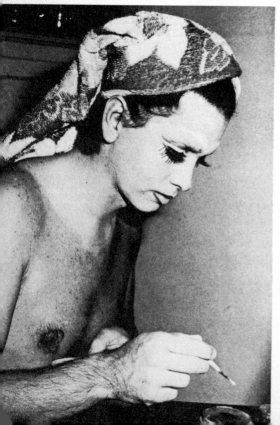

PETER ACKROYD

DRESSING UP

Transvestism and Drag:
The History of an Obsession

with 146 illustrations

THAMES AND HUDSON

ACKNOWLEDGMENTS

Although this is not a scholarly or scientific work (no doubt there are anthropologists, historians and psychiatrists who could modify or expand what I have to say here), I have enlisted the help of many people in its composition.

My especial thanks must go to Barry Kay, whose support and advice have been invaluable in the writing of this book. I should also like to thank Leo Abse, John Ashbery, Roger Baker, Jonathan Benthall, Bruce Chatwin, Homer Dickens, Gillian Freeman, Pat Rogers, A.L. Rowse and Richard Shone. And of course I owe an especial debt to those transvestites and transsexuals who agreed to talk to me and answer my questions.

Printed in Great Britain
by Jarrold and Sons Ltd, Norwich

CONTENTS

1 The Transvestite Community: theories and definitions   9

2 Transvestism Accepted   37

3 Transvestism Rejected   51

4 The Famous Cases   69

5 Transvestism as Performance   89

6 Transvestism in Literature   141

Bibliography   154

Sources of Illustrations   155

Index   156

THE TRANSVESTITE COMMUNITY: THEORIES AND DEFINITIONS

François Timoléon de Choisy, born in 1644, 'was accustomed from childhood to wear petticoats, dresses, corsets and caps'. His mother was a friend of 'Monsieur', the transvestitic Duc d'Orléans, and it is possible that de Choisy was dressed up in order to flatter or please him. He certainly dressed entirely in girls' clothes until the age of ten, and it is reported that he never wore the clothes of his own sex until he was eighteen and enrolled at the Sorbonne.

In the same year that de Choisy obtained the Abbacy of St-Seine, 1663, he appeared as an actress in a Bordeaux theatre. As he records in his *Memoirs*, 'During five months I played in comedy at the theatre of a large city, dressed as a girl; everybody was deceived.' His life thereafter encompassed an extraordinary range of private and public spectacle. It appears that he cross-dressed continually for nine years, appearing as a woman at parties and theatres. He eventually entered a 'marriage of conscience' with a certain Mademoiselle de Charlotte and they lived together for some time, with Charlotte disguised as a male and calling herself 'Monsieur de Maulny'. The Abbé himself went under the name of 'Madame de Sancy'. The strange affair became public knowledge; in a popular verse of the time, it was recorded:

> *In the Faubourg Saint-Marceau*
> *Sancy wears a woman's gown,*
> *Petticoates and furbelow*
> *With which he has amazed the town.*

But the mock marriage came to an end and, after what appears to have been relatively mild social criticism, de Choisy moved to Bourges where he installed himself in a grand house and lived as the 'Comtesse des Barrès'. Here, for a time, he was happy: 'I was gazed at to my heart's content: the novelty of my robes, my diamonds and other finery all attracted attention.'

But the best, and worst, was to come. De Choisy was sent by his superiors to Rome in order to attend the election of Pope Innocent XI in 1676, and it is reported that he dressed as a woman for the ball after the Pope's coronation. The years immediately following this incident are obscure, although it appears that for a time he lived in Italy entirely in female clothes. In 1683 he became suddenly and mysteriously ill, and during his sickness he complained of nightmares concerning 'ne'r-do-wells dressed as women and of conclavistes who were sceptics' – suggesting that his pleasurable and easy acceptance of cross-dressing concealed certain social and religious anxieties. Upon his recovery he seems to have renounced his more unusual activities for a while, and composed a work on the immortality of the soul.

In 1685 he visited Siam in the entourage of Louis XIV's ambassador, and it is reported that 'to a feast in honour of the French visitors, de Choisy went gorgeously arrayed in a feminine evening gown, make-up and jewellery. The Siamese thought it was a European custom of some sort.' Towards the end of his life, de Choisy reverted to his early habit of complete transvestism, and it was while he

(Opposite) *'Don't Play the Heartless One': nineteenth-century lithograph by Tassaert. Cross-dressing is sometimes considered to be sexually titillating*

A young man dressed as a woman. Although the transformation is a striking one, the illusion is rarely complete

(Opposite) *A transvestite taking part in the Mardi Gras celebrations in New Orleans. This annual festival is a rallying-point for transvestites, transsexuals and drag artists from all over the United States*

was dressed as a woman that he wrote his *History of the Church*. Never can a devotional work have been composed in such odd circumstances and, as D'Alembert writes, 'to appreciate the literary value of these ecclesiastical annals it will perhaps suffice to call to mind the picture of an old priest, more than seventy years of age, dressed in a costume unsuited to his age, sex and condition, working on a history of martyrs and anchorites'. De Choisy died in 1724. His is one of the first well-attested cases of true transvestism. But, although his colourful career perhaps matches the conventional image of the male transvestite, the condition itself is of a more substantial and complex nature.

Although transvestism is now considered to be primarily a sexual obsession it has, during its long history, often been associated with sacred ritual and with the expression of social or political dissent. It is a persistent and universal activity; it exists wherever sexual behaviour itself exists, perhaps lying dormant in most human beings; and it is to be found in most cultures and across many centuries. But it still remains fundamentally inexplicable: why is there this repeated need for inversion and disorder?

The subject has been unnecessarily obscured by misapprehensions and superstitions. The word itself evokes the fundamental fact: transvestism is literally the act of cross-dressing, when one sex adopts the clothes of the other. The contemporary, clinical definition of transvestism is more specific: it describes it as an act of cross-dressing which is accompanied by fetishistic obsessions; according to this description, it is a male aberration, of a wholly or predominantly sexual kind. But this is an accurate account only within certain historical and cultural limits – there are male transvestites who are not fetishistic, there are records of female transvestism, and so on. My assumption in this book is a more comprehensive one. Transvestism here describes those occasions when a man puts on a woman's clothes, or a woman adopts a man's, for whatever purpose and with whatever effect. In this context, then, transvestism

should be taken to mean any act of cross-dressing.

Various distinctions, however, still have to be made. Transvestites are not to be confused with trans-sexuals, whose obsessive desire is to assume the genitals and the body of the opposite sex, or with drag artists – who will be discussed separately. These distinctions are central to any understanding of the nature of transvestism since, although trans-sexuals must necessarily pass through a transvestitic phase, cross-dressing is for them a marginal and inconclusive activity. Trans-sexualism is the conviction of biologi-cally normal men and women that they are in reality members of the opposite sex – that they are, in the language of cliché, trapped in the wrong body. Male trans-sexuals, in other

A man cross-dressed, from a visiting card by W. Zoli. The disparity between dress and appearance is sometimes more comic than grotesque

(Left) Violette Moriss, much disapproved of by the Fédération Sportive Feminine for her masculine dress and behaviour

(Opposite) Julian Eltinge, the American transvestite entertainer of the early twentieth century, marrying himself by means of a trick photograph. This is perhaps the ultimate act of narcissism, to which many transvestites aspire

words, conceive of themselves as both female and feminine. Transvestites, on the other hand, are always aware of their male identity and it plays a major role in their activity; it is important to remember that, in all the cases we will discuss, the transvestite priest, rebel or performer assert their maleness – in however camouflaged a state. For male transsexuals the adoption of female clothes is neither an exciting nor an exhibitionistic activity; for male transvestites the alien clothing is itself the most significant element in their cross-dressing.

It is also necessary to distinguish transvestism from drag because, although there are connections to be traced between the two phenomena, they remain fundamentally separate. Drag is primarily a homosexual performance; most transvestites are heterosexual, often married and with children. Again, drag may be a publicly acceptable way for certain homosexual transvestites to relieve their obsession, but instead of implicitly adhering to the prevailing sexual and social codes, as transvestism does, it flouts and breaks them. Drag parodies and mocks women – it is misogynistic both in origin and in intent, which transvestism clearly is not. The contemporary male transvestite wishes to create at least the illusion of femininity – 'to pass' as a woman, either publicly or privately. For him, female clothes are a serious expression of fetishistic or anarchic tendencies. They are not a vehicle for satire at women's expense.

There are, unfortunately, no reliable statistics concerning the incidence of transvestism; it has been suggested, however, that between 1 and 3 per cent of the male population in Britain have transvestitic impulses of various degrees. Male transvestites are rarely effeminate or homosexual. Indeed, most transvestites are firmly heterosexual, and cross-dressing often increases their heterosexual activities; their obsession fuels their sexuality and, at the same time, sexual intercourse with women can seem a way of erasing, or expiating for, embarrassing transvestitic impulses. Transvestites are not, of course, a breed apart. They are generally ordinary people who suffer from an extraordinary compulsion, as baffling to themselves as it is to others. Transvestism is not the exclusive characteristic of any class, type, or society. I have come across an eminent academic who is a transvestite, and one who is mentally retarded.

Nor does transvestism take one easily recognizable form – in fact, it comprises at least two distinct aspects. Some transvestites, for example, are exclusively fetishistic; they dress, in other words, to obtain some kind of sexual arousal. Psychoanalysts believe this to be the dominant mode of transvestism and, indeed, many transvestites remain fixed at this stage, assuaging their obsessions by frequent or intermittent cross-dressing. But there are other transvestites who move out of the fetishistic stage; they cease to be sexually excited by the act of cross-dressing itself, and go on to a more comprehensive form of feminine 'passing'. They dress as women for long periods, appear in public as such and, as one transvestite put it, 'they take their aspirations to femininity seriously, and make a genuine attempt to behave as well as to dress like women'. This might appear to be a latent or unacknowledged form of trans-sexualism – except that, in all cases, the male identity of the transvestite remains intact. But here, on the border between transvestism and transsexualism, specific definitions are neither relevant nor possible. There are transvestites who fantasize about changing their sex, but equally there are other transvestites who are repelled by the idea. Only one thing is clear: it is possible to dress, behave and even think like a woman – as many transvestites do both in public and in private – without in fact being trans-sexual.

(Opposite) *A drag artist reading a 'fanzine'. Drag artists will often take their cue from stereotyped images of women*

(Overleaf) *A trans-sexual in Sydney*

A street-scene in King's Cross, Sydney, a famous district for drag entertainment and trans-sexual prostitution

(Opposite) A drag performer in his dressing-room, working for a Sydney drag revue

One distinction between the two conditions, though, is evident enough. Transvestites can live and work in the social world without at any time revealing their obsessions or displaying their condition. There are lawyers, post-office workers, policemen, farmers, engineers, clergymen and labourers who spend their evenings in women's clothes. Some do so infrequently, and are quite at ease with their conventional male dress and behaviour, but for others masculine clothing (and the attitudes which attend it) imposes an enormous strain which can only be relieved by cross-dressing. One Irish transvestite explained that to be in male clothes was like 'being confined for long periods in one room, as though I had been ill for a long time'.

But despite the relief it affords, most transvestites suffer great anxiety from their condition. Transvestites who are single and alone can endure great misery and isolation, and their impulses may seem horrifyingly unnatural but at the same time unavoidable. Assuming that he has the courage to go into public places and buy the clothes he needs, the transvestite will then 'dress' in his own house, or in a hotel room, and indulge in lonely and often masturbatory fantasies – engaging in fruitless confrontations with his new mirror image. The situation of married transvestites is generally as unsatisfactory. If, as is ordinarily the case, their condition is neither understood nor appreciated by their wives, they will be forced to rent apartments or book into hotels where they can dress unobserved. In those rare situations where wives are either tolerant or sympathetic, the transvestite will dress up in his home and may even entertain mutual friends in that state. He might even become more 'wifely' than his partner.

But it would be a mistake to assume that the transvestite shares the male transsexual's aspiration toward complete femininity. He is indisputably and permanently male and he will, unconsciously or surreptitiously, leave clues to his male gender even within the most complete dressing up. The make-up may not be entirely perfect, the

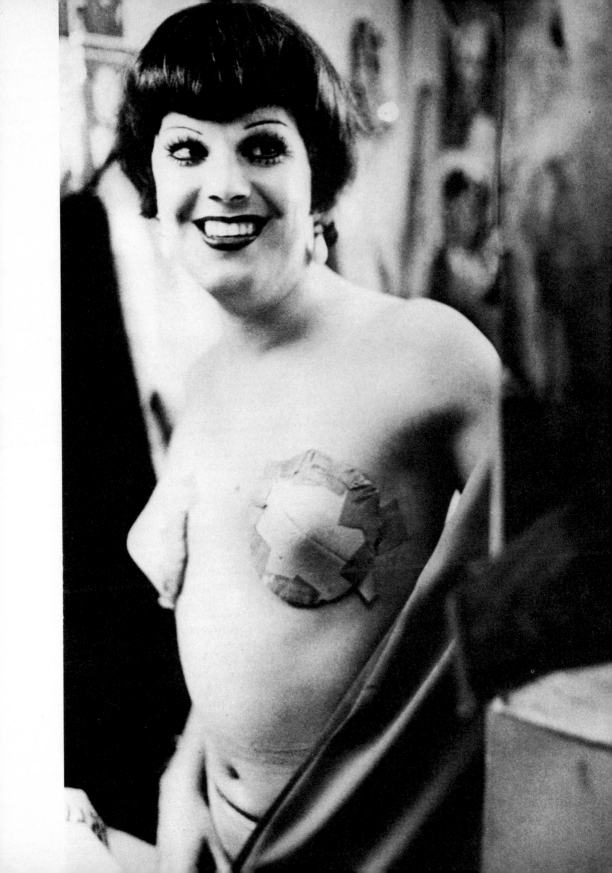

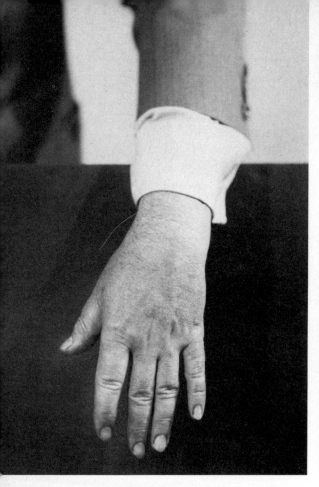
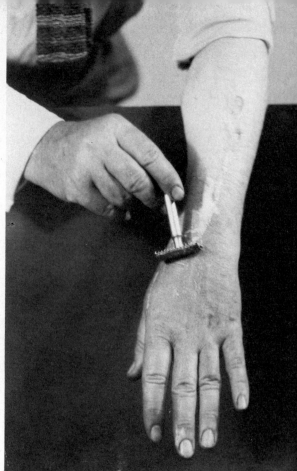

The entertainer Julian Eltinge prepares his hand and arm. Such procedures can be arduous and painful

legs not properly shaved, the voice too low. The well-attested but apparently baffling phenomenon of the normal man who dresses as a crippled woman makes a certain sense in this context: the limp, the mark of imperfection, is a bizarre but effective way of displaying the limits of what might otherwise be a perfect illusion. A transvestite never forgets – and never allows us to forget – that he is a man in woman's clothes.

There are, of course, fetishistic transvestites who have no interest in entering the public domain – their obsession is best satisfied in secret, as it is with those who limit their cross-dressing to the adoption of feminine underwear, and their best audience themselves. But there are many transvestites who, having mastered the guilt and anxiety which their cross-dressing induces, have an

Transvestites themselves are not forth-coming about the nature of their obsession; most of them have no interest in discussing or explaining the nature or context of their activities. This may be because of the inherent narcissism and auto-eroticism involved, but it may also be that the unwillingness or inability of transvestites to define their condition is a direct consequence of its inva-sive, irrational nature. It becomes, literally, indescribable.

If transvestites do attempt to explain the origin or nature of their condition, it is generally in the vaguest of terms. A constant reference, though, is to its longevity. Most transvestites locate their obsession in their infancy, as an unmanageable and threaten-ing 'disease' which haunted and often ruined their youth. The sexual nature of their transvestism is sometimes explicitly dis-cussed – 'When I dress it feels as if I have a continual orgasm' – although many trans-vestites, out of embarrassment or genuine dis-interest, minimize the sexual and fetishistic elements of their cross-dressing. Other factors can also be involved: some trans-vestites will explain how they turn their dressing into a kind of ritual, putting on their clothes in a specific and pre-ordained sequence. Others will wear only certain fabrics. But for most transvestites, cross-dressing is simply a question of doing the thing they do – and being allowed to do it.

This does not imply, though, that the majority of transvestites are happy with their activity. Most of them would abandon it if they were able to (in this respect they differ from other minority groups), and often attempt to sublimate it in the pursuit of sports and other masculine activities. Even those men who have been cross-dressing for a number of years still find the phenomenon to be both threatening and divisive. And for those who have the support of neither family nor friends, it can become acutely oppressive.

Transvestites, especially in their youth, need great courage and determination to withstand the pressures which are involved. They characteristically find their condition distressing, mysterious and yet inescapable;

overwhelming desire to 'pass' in public as women. There is a variety of motives for such overt display. There is the sheerly exhibi-tionistic purpose – to prove how attractive and desirable a woman the transvestite can become. Alternatively, some transvestites only want to be recognized as women *by* other women; others want to be 'read' (the term for penetrating their disguise) only when they sanction it, since they derive a great deal of their pleasure from fooling and then surprising others. Certain transvestites do not care whether they are 'read' or not; for them cross-dressing can become an act of palpable defiance towards a society which imposes absurdly rigid sexual stereotypes. Such transvestites, still very much in a mi-nority, will often exaggerate the disparity between their native sex and their dress.

A transvestite visiting a beautician's for regular depilation

alcoholism and severe depression are often the result. The human waste involved is enormous, and the potential of any human life should not have to be injured or destroyed by a condition which is neither harmful in itself nor dangerous to others.

The attitude of the transvestite's family can be crucial in this respect. Many transvestites marry in the belief that cohabitation with a woman will cure them of their obsession; and those wives who have been told of their husband's transvestism are often convinced that they themselves can effect a cure. Both assumptions are mistaken, and as a consequence the attitude of most wives towards their husbands' condition is unfavourable. Many wives wrongly assume that their husbands are homosexual, while others feel that their own sexuality and attractiveness have been placed in doubt. One transvestite, a farmer who regularly travels to London in order to pass publicly as a woman, told me that his wife is 'sickened' by his condition and refuses to allow him to cross-dress in the house. And so when his obsession becomes too strong to withstand, he simply leaves home for two or three days and assumes his alternative identity. It ought also to be put on record that other transvestites believe that their wives are envious of their clothes and their feminine appearance, although this is in fact unlikely to be the case. But it is certainly true that a small number of wives are sympathetic towards their husband's transvestism. In some instances they actively help in the buying of clothes and in the process of dressing. This might on some occasions be a quasi-lesbian, or man-hating, activity but on others it is a reflection of genuine compassion.

The attitudes of male transvestites to women are complex, but the primary response is one of admiration or envy. It has been suggested that transvestites cross-dress in order to identify themselves more and more closely with women, and to pay them the ultimate compliment of abandoning temporarily the male sex. There may be some truth in this, but the female image which transvestites admire and copy is not one that most women would recognize. The clothes which transvestites characteristically wear, for example, are drab in nature and old-fashioned in design. It is possible that the image of femininity which the transvestite adopts is one that is derived from his earliest memories of his mother or female relations. The nondescript nature of the clothes may also represent a kind of desperate conformism, in the attempt to pass unnoticed by avoiding the extravagance of, for example, drag artists. But the clothes may simply be an aspect of age – there may well be younger transvestites who will soon be dressing in the image of the 'liberated' woman. There is nothing 'liberated' about the majority of transvestites, however, who are overtly feminine and sometimes self-consciously coy when they are 'dressed'.

This overt femininity may be a defensive strategy, a kind of protective camouflage for the sexuality and fetishism inherent in certain forms of cross-dressing, or equally it may represent a genuine division within the personality of the transvestite. 'Barbara Barrie', for example, writes of herself – in a magazine for transvestites – in the most over-determined manner: 'Barbara managed to slip lady-like into her car, adjusting skirts over nylon clad – dare I say it!! – shapely legs, and was off. Driving en femme proved to be a great thrill. . . . It was nice to sit down with skirt discreetly pulled over closed legs, have a lady-like smoke, and sip a bitter lemon.'

It would be easy to be ironic or dismissive about this kind of writing, but its over-elaborate femininity is a melancholy reminder of how deeply the sexual stereotypes are ingrained within our culture. Transvestites are helplessly confined in the roles which have been assigned to them, and conform to them in a compulsive act of homage.

Their submersion in sexist culture partly explains their attitude towards homosexuals. The Beaumont Society, the British organization for transvestites and trans-sexuals, actively excludes them from its meetings – and there are very few heterosexual transvestites who show any interest in, or sympathy with, their homosexual colleagues. This is perhaps because of a fear of latent homosexuality within their own transvestitic impulses but, in any event, it is certainly the case that homosexual transvestites are the most misunderstood and neglected of all; they are rejected by heterosexual transvestites, ridiculed by homosexuals, and generally find themselves lost in that small space between the minorities.

Some transvestites, however, cross-dress with ease and security, aware of but not troubled by their ambiguous status in the public world. There are also societies for transvestites in many countries, which actively assist in the process of 'coming-out'. But these societies are by no means homogeneous; transvestism itself bears the distinctive marks of each culture from which it springs. In Japan, for example, where cross-dressing has played a major and persistent role in the theatre and where the established religion encourages a form of androgyny, transvestism is both widespread and acceptable.

It is paradoxical that transvestism can also flourish in male-dominated and overtly chauvinistic cultures. In Australia, for example, male transvestites are more acceptable than male homosexuals. The curious working of sexual stereotypes is evident here: a masculine or 'machismo' culture may not easily reconcile itself to male inversion, and can only deal with such inversion when it is camouflaged as a 'female' condition. Transvestites have exiled themselves from the male world, and can be treated as surrogate women – thereby ceasing to be a threat. Indeed many Australian homosexuals 'dress up', although they have neither transvestitic nor trans-sexual impulses.

But in certain societies where the male presence has been dominant for long periods, transvestism has been rationalized and made economically viable as a form of prostitution. And so – in Italy, for example – it remains a recognizable and acceptable deviation, but only within strict limits. The central phenomenon of obsessive or fetishistic transvestism

is little known and little discussed. In Northern Europe, on the other hand, social attitudes towards transvestism are characteristically 'liberal' and there is very little overt discrimination against transvestites in Denmark, Holland, Sweden and Germany. In America and England the response to transvestism is more ambiguous. Although there is little evidence of social or legal repression, the tradition of comic drag in both countries has dominated public recognition of cross-dressing – and transvestites have as a consequence been seen as freakish or merely funny.

There are also transvestitic publications in many countries, some pornographic and fetishistic but others informative and intelligently written. These publications will be discussed elsewhere, but it is worth noticing in this context one universal element in transvestitic literature: the photograph. Transvestites send in photographs of themselves which are duly published. Some of them are pornographic, displaying erections within female underwear and so on, but the majority of them are affectingly simple portraits of transvestites, standing or sitting, smiling directly at the camera. Their 'femme' names are printed underneath, as if their artificial act of rebirth is one which only the artificiality of the camera can represent and sanctify. Barry Kay's unique collection of photographs, some of which appeared in his book *The Other Women*, gives a very clear sense of the plaintive mimicry of the transvestite disguise; his images are a confirmation of the extraordinariness of the sexual and social change which has taken place, but they are also pictures of isolation.

Since that time when transvestism was first defined as a specific condition, in the early part of this century, there have been a number of theories designed to account for its persistence and universality. The most sustained and important work of this kind has been done by psychologists and, although many of their speculations are now of historical rather than analytical interest, they provide an apt representation of changing attitudes towards the subject.

Before the advent of clinical accounts, transvestism was generally associated with other deviancies, often as the outward sign of some deeper and more threateningly anti-social behaviour. It was often confused, for example, with sorcery or with homosexuality – although the earliest 'medical' definitions were hardly more precise. Cross-dressing was seen only as a symptom of acute mental instability. Jean Esquirol, a French doctor who specialized in mental illnesses, diagnosed transvestism in *Des maladies mentales* (1838) as a form of *dementia praecox*. Carl Westphal, a German clinician, described it in *Archiv für Psychiatrie* (1876) as an 'anti-pathic sexual instinct' related to severe mental disorder.

This unhappy situation is one that has changed in only modest ways and, when we take account of the analytical descriptions of transvestism, it ought to be remembered that they are generally culled from the 'case-histories' of 'patients'. The theoretical literature, although more dispassionate and lucid than anything which comes before it, is still marked by the implicit assumption that transvestism is a disease with recognizable symptoms and one that is susceptible to curative procedures.

Even Krafft-Ebing, who made a detailed study of transvestism – which he called 'dress-fetishism' – in *Psycopathia sexualis* (1886), saw it as the first stage in the onset of *metamorphosis sexualis paranoica*. He devised four categories for the condition: the simple obsession for wearing women's clothes, which is specifically fetishistic in nature; the passive homosexual's desire to be seen as a woman; heterosexuals who cross-dress because of marked or marginal her-maphroditism; and, finally, those people who because of their 'delusion of sexual transfor-mation' genuinely desire to adopt the appearance and sentiments of the opposite sex. This classification may be simplistic, but it marks one of the first attempts to separate transvestism from homosexuality and trans-sexuality – although trans-sexualism itself was not to be clearly defined until 1949.

A transvestite, or perhaps a fetishistic trans-sexual – a typical photograph from a transvestite magazine

But Krafft-Ebing's suggestion that cross-dressing may be indirectly related to sexual hermaphroditism raises a question which has bedevilled the discussion of transvestism. Is it characteristically the result of cultural and familial circumstances, as most analytical writers suggest, or is it a condition that can be linked to hereditary factors? The possibility that transvestism is, in certain cases, associated with schizophrenia and even psychosis suggests that there may – occasionally – be chemical or biological forces at work in its inception.

The actual term 'transvestism' was first used by Magnus Hirschfeld in *Die Transvestiten* (1925). He extended and refined Krafft-Ebing's schematic description by suggesting that there were heterosexual transvestites (35 per cent of the total number), homosexual transvestites (also 35 per cent), narcissists and, finally, asexual cross-dressers whose transvestism was accompanied by impotence and feminine activity.

This analysis, although by no means rudimentary, is clearly unsatisfactory; it is anecdotal and excessively schematic, as though the act of naming were equivalent to the process of understanding. Havelock Ellis placed the phenomenon of transvestism in a broader context in *Eonism* (1923), in which cross-dressing is named after the Chevalier D'Eon (who is discussed elsewhere) – thus forming a trinity of eponymous aberrations with sadism and masochism. Ellis's analysis of transvestism is more interesting because he does not view it solely in the context of mental aberration. He even suggests at one point that cross-dressing 'may be the survival of an ancient and natural tendency of primitive man', an insight which has proved of great value; the emphasis here on its potential naturalness – and therefore of its historical and essentially inexplicable nature – is one that removes him from his contemporaries who regarded transvestism as a disease or a 'sexual anomaly'.

(Opposite) *Prince William, later Duke of Gloucester (1743–1805), as a small boy*

Ellis also suggests that transvestism is a 'sexo-aesthetic inversion', a 'modification of normal heterosexuality' in the sense that the transvestite is so attracted to women that he wishes to become permanently or intermittently identified with them. His impulse 'springs out of admiration and affection for the opposite sex' and, when cross-dressed, the transvestite (or 'eonist') 'achieves a completely emotional identification which is sexually abnormal but aesthetically correct'. And so this advanced and aesthetically shaped condition tends to occur 'among people who are educated, refined, sensitive and reserved'.

This is not, in fact, the case, and Havelock Ellis's misjudgment here is part of a larger confusion. It is perhaps only in Freud's essays on human sexuality that transvestism emerges into a fitful light. It does so only indirectly since Freud never gives an explicit account of the phenomenon but its presence can be traced, for example, in his essay on sexual aberrations, 'Die sexuellen Abirrungen' in *Drei Abhandlungen zur Sexualtheorie* (1905): 'In all the cases we have examined we have established the fact that future inverts, in the earliest years of their childhood, pass through a phase of very intense but short-lived fixation on a woman (who is usually their mother) and that, after leaving this behind they identify themselves with a woman and take themselves as their sexual object.' This overt identification with the female, together with the auto-eroticism involved, is clearly of relevance to the condition of the adult transvestite. Male transvestites themselves speak of their condition as deriving from infant memories and obsessions, whether through some traumatic experience of loss or betrayal or through the fixation upon an individual garment. That garment may have acted as a safe and unthreatening substitute for the female body which the infant desires; Havelock Ellis's suggestion that the transvestite wishes to be permanently identified with a woman takes on new relevance if we assume the woman in question to be his mother.

27

The Prince of Wales, later Edward VIII, at the age of two

Julian Eltinge, as man and woman

Indeed, infantile elements run deeply through transvestism. It is an auto-erotic and generally masturbatory activity, often performed in front of a mirror where the bodily image takes precedence over the social and objective relations of the adult world. The wearing of women's clothes, in addition, charges the body of the transvestite with a diffuse but powerful sexual excitement – as though it were a febrile re-enactment of the skin-to-skin contact with the mother which he enjoyed in his infancy. He has never been able to erase or repress the mother's warm acknowledgment that 'you are part of me' (a notion often deliberately emphasised when mothers dress their male infants as little girls), and so it returns in bizarre and incongruous forms. The gesture of cross-dressing may, in these cases, be both a way of alleviating the permanent psychic discomfort of male clothing and a means of reuniting the transvestite with the image of the mother which he has retained. Magnus Hirschfeld has noted, for example, that certain transvestites dream of maternal happiness and try to re-enact it: some going so far as to dress as pregnant women.

There is another aspect of Freud's analysis which is of peculiar relevance to the transvestitic phenomenon. 'The child believes that it is only unworthy female persons that have lost their genitals – females who, in all probability, were guilty of inadmissible impulses similar to his own. Women whom he respects, like his mother, retain a penis for a long time' (*Fetischismus*, 1928). The image of the mother which the adult transvestite recreates in his own dressing is that of a 'phallic woman', an identification which he is in a peculiarly strong position to sustain. But, also, when the infant realises that his mother is without a penis, a whole sequence of defensive strategies begins to work: '. . . if a woman has been castrated, then his own possession of a penis was in danger . . . the fetish is a substitute for the woman's (the mother's) penis that the little boy once believed in and – for reasons familiar to us – does not want to give up . . .'. Cross-dressing is clearly a bulwark against these infantile

Julian Eltinge with his mother. The resemblance is striking

feelings of threat and loss. The spectacle of the man dressed as a woman is both a re-enactment of the mother possessing a penis, and an image which explicitly denies the subsequent knowledge of her castration and all the anxieties which that induces. The female clothes which the transvestite wears might in themselves be seen as a symbol of castration – they are flowing, not bifurcated – and yet his penis, the real centre of his obsession, is secure beneath. This camouflage therefore becomes a way of resolving the conflicts and fears of childhood. As Freud puts it, 'the horror of castration has set up a memorial to itself in the creation of this substitute'.

The work of Robert Stoller, an American psychiatrist, is relevant here since his *Sex and Gender* (1968) has become an authoritative text in the study of transvestism and trans-sexualism. He explores there the role of the phallic woman in the transvestitic disguise, and his account of the transvestite's identity is particularly illuminating. He distinguishes between sex, male or female, and gender, masculine or feminine, which is culturally determined. The male trans-sexual declares himself to be both female and feminine, but the transvestite's assertion is that 'I am feminine but I am also a male.' This is, according to Stoller, 'a very efficient way of handling very strong feminine identification without his masculinity being threatened'.

It should be evident by now that the available literature is concerned only with male transvestism; indeed female transvestism, according to Stoller, does not exist. Women may, of course, have transvestitic impulses (we see them at work every day in the fashion pages of the newspapers) but they cannot be transvestites because 'men's clothes have no erotic value whatsoever'. Women who live and dress as men are described by Stoller as 'female trans-sexuals'. I suspect, however, that this analysis is too narrow to be entirely correct, and that male clothing has no 'erotic value' because of its ready availability for women within our culture. In other circumstances, it might well acquire fetishistic qualities for certain women and it would no doubt be possible, on the basis of infantile females' belief in their own 'castration', to construct a plausible etiology for female transvestism.

But since the male transvestite is Stoller's primary theme, he goes on to suggest, in part following Freud, that transvestism provides a complex and successful defensive structure. Female clothing becomes a desirable and necessary substitute for the female sexual being, and by cross-dressing the transvestite defends himself against what he senses to be the implicit threat posed by female bodies. *They* may be castrated but he, although firmly identified with their image, is not; he is a better woman. Such beliefs also suggest a kind of exhibitionism: the overt display of inappropriate clothing is an indirect way of drawing attention to the penis which lies underneath.

And so transvestism, in Stoller's account, resurrects 'a desired sense of masculinity and maleness' in the very form in which it had once been threatened. Perhaps the small boy was dressed as a girl by his mother, either to punish or simply to feminize him; or perhaps

the small child became over-attached to a female who later abandoned him, or encroached upon his identity in some traumatic way. And 'by a remarkable tour-de-force he takes the original humiliation and converts it into an active process of sexual mastery and pleasure'.

This is a perceptive account which, in part, explains the prevalence in transvestitic pornography of ferocious images of big-breasted, high-heeled women brandishing long, curled whips. The dominant mistress of such fantasies resembles the image of the original woman whom the transvestite memorializes in his dressing up. And, by a strange inversion, the transvestite himself can become the phallic woman who once threatened to rob him of his identity.

Although this structure of feeling has the innocent inevitability of instinct behind it, it can nevertheless evoke guilt and anxiety. The over-identification with the phallic woman, or with the dowdy woman who is also the mother, comes to represent an indirect form of incest: the transvestite's performance suggests that 'I love the mother who is still part of me, and am sexually aroused by her', and this in turn provokes masochistic demands for humiliation and punishment. That is why sado-masochistic fantasies of every sort play a large part in the pornography of transvestism. 'Forced dressing', when the transvestite is ordered into female clothes by a domineering female, plays a similar role: if he cross-dresses against his will, he bears no responsibility for his actions and is thus vicariously relieved of his guilt.

The auto-erotic nature of transvestism also marks a retreat into infantile fantasy. The transvestite has, to use Jacques Lacan's terminology, withdrawn from the symbolic phase of adult development and returned, helplessly and instinctively, to the imaginary. This auto-eroticism is one indication of the fact that transvestism has very little to do with the need for sexual relationships; it can co-exist equally with homosexuality, heterosexuality and bisexuality since it has no real connection with object choices of that kind. According to Magnus Hirschfeld, the sexual satisfaction involved in cross-dressing is less intense than the mental satisfaction to be derived from it. This may be only partly true, in the sense that transvestitic fetishism is obviously sexual in nature, but of all deviations transvestism is the most 'aesthetic' or cerebral. The feminine fantasies involved, and the associated sensations of secret strength and power, suggest a disequilibrium between the mental and physical constitutions of the transvestite. It is even possible that the masculine component of the transvestite's psyche is aroused by the feminine component – and so on.

It is wise, however, to be wary of generalizations about 'split personalities'. The behaviour of transvestites may bear some resemblance to that of schizophrenics, but it has to be remembered that transvestites are externalizing, and in many cases successfully coping with, their disharmonious tendencies. To suggest otherwise is to condemn transvestism as another form of mental disorder. In fact, I have read one description of transvestism, in John Bancroft's *Deviant Sexual Behaviour*, that practically amounts to a sentence of death: '. . . it represents completely abnormal personality developments of the severest kind, on a psychopathic basis, which are contiguous with well-known phenomena in the region of the psychoses'. One of the results of such observations can be attempts at 'cure' as severe as the diagnosis itself: 'At the beginning of each session an injection of apomorphine was given and the patient told to cross-dress in his usual manner. He was urged to continue the ritual and look at himself in a mirror whilst vomiting and nausea continued.' Transvestites were also asked to 'stand naked on a wired mat through which the shock could be delivered'.

Once we have discarded the necessarily pejorative connections with mental illness, and its attendant 'cures', it must, of course, be admitted that many transvestites dwell within two separate personae. They call themselves by their 'femme' name – Alan may become Pamela, Paul becomes Joyce – and

A woman partisan in the Balkans. The requirements of a sexist culture have often meant that a woman must dress as a man before seeming martial or aggressive

will often refer to their male identities in the third person. It is also the case that many transvestites, when dressed, are more feminine than the most female female – and that other transvestites find it necessary to behave in a theatrically and aggressively masculine way when dressed in male clothes. Transvestism can thus be a natural and justifiable response to the intolerable burdens which the playing of conventional sexual roles imposes upon certain people, whose ambivalent sexual natures are

(Overleaf) *Transvestites at the New Orleans Mardi Gras*

31

'Woman's Emancipation' from Punch *(1851)*

ill-suited to the demands of cultural stereotyping.

This suggests the larger perspective in which transvestism should be located. Dress has always been worn for the purposes of protection and ornamentation, but it is generally now adopted in order to project the wearer's appropriate place in the social and moral order of the community. When men wore top hats and frock-coats, a phallically slim and sombre uniform, at the same time as women wore uselessly elaborate lace and crinoline, a definite statement was being made about the nature of nineteenth-century society and the economic role of the sexes within it. Transvestites abrogate all of these pervasive but unacknowledged codes, and by denying the symbolism invested in the clothing of their sex they break some of the most deeply-held beliefs about the male role and the constraints of a male-dominated society.

It could be said that they change the nature of the fetishism involved – they transform a public symbol into a private one (it might be pointed out in this connection that Hitler's appreciation of ample skirts, puffed sleeves and the 'Gretchen style' represents a private fetish, a kind of infantilism and sentimentality, which had public consequences) at the same time as they change a useful function into a useless one, a communal sense of responsibility and order into a theatrical sense of display and

pleasurable sensation. On the other hand, cross-dressing may simply be taken at face value: as a harmless and often colourful way of alleviating those tensions which social and family life may induce.

But it has often been said that transvestism has no future. In America and Europe, in the age of unisex and punk, it seems an old-fashioned and almost moralistic obsession which will survive only as long as men and women are formally distinguished in their dress and their behaviour. There is a certain truth in this – after all, in contemporary China it must be difficult to cross-dress effectively – but only a partial one. The clothes of both sexes often converge only to separate again (*Punch*'s attack on 'Shemale' costumes was, after all, made in the 1850s) but, more importantly, fetishism and obsessive sexuality will survive changes in fashion. The obsessive aspect of cross-dressing will only be dissipated if it becomes a more public and acceptable form of bodily expression – and this seems unlikely. It is also possible that the growing awareness of trans-sexuality will diminish the incidence of transvestism; there are certain transvestites who are latent trans-sexuals, and for these marginal cross-dressers medical procedures may become of more importance than dressing up.

But this is merely speculation and, like every other analysis of the causes and conditions of transvestism recorded in this chapter, open to doubt and ambiguity. I came to the subject as an outsider, and have in a sense remained one since it is still for me a puzzlingly various and often contradictory phenomenon. All that can be said with certainty is that it represents, in public and visible form, the pure spirit of difference. If it were possible to dispel the miasma of moral and sexual taboo which surrounds so essentially simple and instinctive an activity, transvestism could take a small but interesting place in the history of human expression.

(Opposite) 'One of New York's mannish girls out for a morning "breather"'

34

2
TRANSVESTISM ACCEPTED

Transvestism has not always been considered a subversive or especially deviant practice. It may be difficult to imagine societies in which sexual ambiguity of this most uncompromising kind could be accepted and even revered, but anthropologists and social historians have recorded the incidence of cross-dressing in diverse cultures – palaeo-Asiatic, North American, African, European – and across many centuries.

There have been cultures in which transvestism has been institutionalized, and transvestites themselves given generic status as a kind of honorary third sex. Among certain American Indian tribes, for example, the *berdaches* were those men who wore women's clothes and engaged in specifically feminine activities. Westermarck reported in 1917 that 'In nearly every part of North America there seem to have been, since ancient times, men dressing themselves in the clothes and performing the functions of women . . .'. Indeed the Dakota Indians had an expression, 'fine possessions like a *berdache*'s', which suggests that their social role was clearly defined.

The existence of this minority, living alongside the two sexes, is well attested: among the Cocopa Indians, males who showed feminine characteristics were dressed in women's clothes and known as *e L ha*. In Tahiti, transvestites who dressed permanently as women were known as *mahoos*; in Brazil as *cudinas*; among the Californian Indians as *i-wa-musp*; and among the Aztecs and Incas as *bardage*. It has been suggested that some of these men–women earned their living as homosexual prostitutes, but for many of them this permanent state of cross-dressing seems to have been both natural and acceptable. It is impossible now to ascertain

their precise sexual identity – they may have been heterosexual transvestites or latent trans-sexuals. It is also possible that this form of cross-dressing was one which allowed early societies to harness homosexuality as a constructive social force: for example the *berdaches* were, as Ruth Benedict puts it, 'leaders in women's occupations'. But it is clear that, for whatever reason, transvestites played a large and well-integrated role within certain societies; although attitudes to them might well have been ambivalent (the 'husband' of such a man–woman was often the target of ridicule), they were afforded social and legal status.

But transvestism also marks a dramatic and even terrifying change in a human being, and it would be wrong to suggest that it is always marked by the passivity and social conformity of the *berdaches*. Cross-dressing has often been the sign of an extraordinary destiny. In many shamanistic cultures, transvestites are regarded as sorcerers or visionaries who, because of their double nature as men dressed as women, are sources of divine authority within the community. This is not a wholly archaic superstition; Jan Morris, a trans-sexual, has written in *Conundrum* that 'the black people of Africa made me feel that there was to my condition an element of privilege'.

It is not surprising that this double nature should be seen as a sign of the sacred, when we consider the androgynous or at least bisexual nature of the deities which are worshipped. If, as the Creation myths assert, Chaos – or the unity of undifferentiated sexuality – is the progenitor of all life, then the separate sexes represent a falling off from that original fecundity. Androgyny, in which the two sexes co-exist in one form and which the transvestite priest imitates in his own person, is an original state of power. In Africa, for example, one of the principal deities of the Abomey pantheon is Lisa-

(Opposite) *A Crow Indian, reputedly the last of the* berdaches

Maron, a figure which incorporates both man and woman; the great god Shango can be represented as either male or female; and contemporary shamans in Brazil worship Yansan, who is the 'man–woman'. In a more familiar context, Adam, the father of the human race, is described in some sources as an androgynous figure. And Maximus the Confessor, as quoted by Scotus Erigena, asserts that Christ at his Resurrection 'was neither man nor woman'. We are dealing here with something that is deeply rooted in the human psyche.

Androgyny is the central aspect of the deities of vegetation and fertility, and it is here that transvestism comes into its own as an essential and unique form of worship. Macrobius reports that male priests dressed as women in honour of the Bearded Aphrodite of Cyprus; on the same island, the cult of Ariadne (originally a fertility cult) was marked by a ceremony in which a boy was dressed in female clothes and proceeded to enact all the symptoms of labour and birth. At Roman harvest rituals, the gods of agriculture were addressed 'sive deus sis, sive dea'. This persistent identification of cross-dressing with ideas of growth and rebirth is one which, as we will see later, marks most fertility rites and it is one which still persists in contemporary harvest festivals.

It is never quite clear whether this universal myth of the androgynous, procreative gods is meant to represent an aspect of human reality, or of another reality completely removed from the human dimension. That is why transvestism can be such a powerfully ambiguous force, and why the transvestitic shaman was considered a healer, a chosen one of God. The power to change sex, or at least to represent that process by adopting alien clothes, links the shaman to the double-sexed and self-sufficient deities who use him as their mouthpiece.

The shaman does, in a sense, incorporate the divine presence; his body is a receptacle of spirits with which, in ecstatic communion, he pleads and fights on behalf of his people. Often the initiate is summoned in dream to

A Sakpota dancer in Dahomey. Cross-dressing was often used to appease malign spirits

(Opposite) *A celebrant at a ritual in Brazil, in honour of Shango, the thunder god of the Yorubas. The deity itself could be portrayed as either a male or female figure, and the male celebrants cross-dressed in his or her honour*

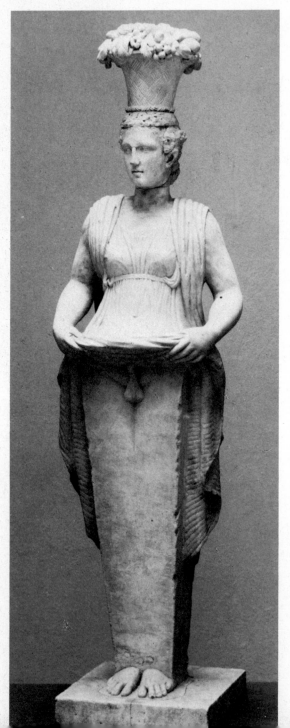

(Opposite) *'The Land of Hermaphrodites', from* Le Livre des merveilles, *fifteenth century*

A Greek hermaphroditic statue. Hermaphroditism was characteristically considered to be the original state of humankind, of which cross-dressing is a relic and a memorial

become a shaman, by a command which he dare not refuse; sometimes his vocation emerges through the onset of madness or of serious sickness. In all cases the shaman must be reborn before he can assume his proper role, and to mark that rebirth he may assume female clothes. As Ioan Lewis puts it in *Ecstatic Religion*, '... the initial experience withdraws the victim from the secure world of society and of ordered existence, and exposes him directly to those forces which, though they may be held to uphold the social order, are also ultimately threatening'. What could be more conformist than the clothes which mark sexual gender, and yet what could be more 'threatening' than the uses to which they are put by the transvestitic shaman?

Of course, it would be wrong to suggest that all shamans are transvestites (or that all transvestites are shamans), but the persistence of cross-dressing among primitive priests is well attested and worthy of notice. According to Herodotus, Scythian shamans who spoke and dressed as women were highly honoured and feared. Among the Chukchee of North-East Asia, even the sexually normal shamans dressed permanently in women's clothes. James Frazer reports in *The Golden Bough* that in the Pelew Islands, 'a goddess chooses a man, not a woman, for her minister and her inspired mouthpiece ... He wears female attire, he carries a piece of gold on his neck, he labours like a woman in the tano fields.' And, Frazer goes on to say, 'this is a custom widely spread among savages'.

The priests of Artemis at Ephesus are reputed to have worn female clothing. Among the Sea Dyaks of Borneo, every *manang* or shaman was a transvestite. Young boys among the Mohave Indians who were destined to become shamans were dressed as women, and the Omaha Indians considered all transvestites to be sacred. Among the Teso of central Africa, the medicine-men dressed as women. The shamans of the Asiatic Eskimos cross-dressed. In India, the Vallabha sect, devotees of Krishna, dressed as women. Transvestite priests were common among the Aztecs, the Incas and the Mayas

Rajshahi, from Bengal. Bisexuality seen as a state of self-sufficiency and power: hence the cross-dressing of many priests and shamans

(only to be tortured and burnt to death by their Christian conquerors). Men had to dress up before they could take part in the rites of Hercules at Rome (Hercules himself spent three years dressed as a woman at the court of Omphale, Queen of Lydia). Among the Yakut of aboriginal Siberia, 'black' or destructive shamans dressed in women's clothes – and it is as well to mention here that, during the medieval witch trials, it was attested that one of the marks of a sorcerer was the ability to change sex. In the Congo, the sacrificial priest dressed as a woman and was known as 'Grandmother'. Reports, of the 1870s and 1930s, describe the priests (*bissu*) of the Celebes who live and dress as women.

What possible explanations are there for the persistence and apparent universality of transvestism as a sacred and powerful condition? It has been suggested that the male priest dressed as a woman symbolizes the confluence of earth, the female principle, and sky, the male. It has also been suggested that transvestite priests are a relic of some earlier cult matriarchy, in which the clothes of women are the symbols of the established order. On the other hand, cross-dressing has been taken to represent the communal order of 'Mother Nature', as opposed to the hierarchies of male-dominated society. But the fact that transvestism is often associated with hysteria and psychic disturbance within the shaman points to another possible explanation: it may be that the adoption of female clothing is a dramatic way of reconciling sexual tensions within the individual shaman and, through his ritual enactments, within the community itself. It must also be remembered that transvestism, is in appearance if not in motivation, a threateningly asexual phenomenon (which is why, in modern civilization, it arouses fears of castration and so on); in tribal societies, where sexuality is not repressed in conventional forms, the transvestitic shaman might well represent the absence of sexuality, a negative image which could induce a kind of sacred terror and thus stabilize the relations between the sexes. We need not, I think, speculate on the sexual identity of the

Albanian virgins living as men after objecting to being married. Female cross-dressing is often the mark of those women who have rejected conventional social and familial structures. The Amazonian myth suggests just how threatening this phenomenon can seem to a male-dominated society

shaman; in contemporary cultures, the priests of androgynous cults – as in the worship of Yansan in Brazil – are effeminate homosexuals, but there is no reason to believe that this was a necessary or even prevalent condition.

It must further be remembered that the clothes of the transvestitic shaman are in no sense peripheral to his magical activities, the outward signs of some inward grace. The clothes are important *in themselves*, as much a part of the man as his heart or his soul. When a Mongol, for example, was very ill his best clothes were spread around his bed in order to tempt back the wavering soul. Clothes have certain innate magical properties: Ernest Crawley reports that, at the Zulu Black Ox sacrifice, men wear women's girdles in order to provoke rain. It used to be a custom among old Arabs that, if a man were stung by a scorpion, he would immediately put on a woman's bracelets and ear-rings. And, of course, cross-dressing was also used to deceive malignant spirits.

And so for a man to wear women's clothes is an act of practical and spiritual, rather than sexual, significance. By altering outward appearance in this radical way, and so inverting all of the customs of sexual differentiation, an individual or tribe acquires certain powers which are thought to affect the external world: to cure a wound that would otherwise fester, to elicit rain from a clear sky. By symbolically discarding the predetermined vestments of his own sex, the shaman approaches the power of the androgynous gods and finds fresh access to life, strength and health.

(Overleaf)
A transvestitic shaman invokes the spirit of Kali

Heviosso's priest, in Abomey, dances in women's clothes

Queen Hat-shepsūt in the custume of a pharaoh, from her temple at Deir el Bahri, Thebes; Egyptian sculpture, Eighteenth Dynasty (1485 BC). The 'bearded woman' is a popular figure of folklore, often associated with power, saintliness or wisdom

(Opposite) *Boys undergoing an initiation ceremony in an Angolan tribe*

Thus during many rites of passage – at the great ceremonies of circumcision, marriage and death – transvestism plays a major and natural role. It represents the rebirth of life and strength; and if the binary classifications of male–female can be altered by symbolic reversal, so can those of life–death, single–married, human–animal. Frazer records that Masai boys, after circumcision, wear women's clothes and ornaments until their wounds are healed. Among the Namshi, the boys are dressed in skirts and necklaces during the rites of initiation. When an Egyptian boy was circumcised, he paraded in female garments. These transvestitic preparations for entry into the masculine world are prefigured in the myth of Achilles, who lived and dressed as a woman at the court of Lycomedes in Scyros before acquiring his martial skills. It seems that cross-dressing can represent a kind of self-sufficiency, and from that self-sufficiency come personal power and courage. The adoption and subsequent abandonment of women's clothing are also, of course, a decisive way of rejecting the world of women.

Since transvestism represents a change in oneself, and can provoke a change in nature, it plays an important part in harvest and fertility rites. Indeed it was through the overt identification with such festivals that cross-dressing earned its reputation as a symbol of sexual licence and buffoonery. In fact, its sacred function is scarcely recorded, and the rites of which we have descriptions are merely the relics of much more primitive ceremonies. At the vine growers' festival, the Athenian Oschophoria, two boys dressed in women's clothes and carried a vine stock in procession. At the Argive festival of Hybristika, the men adopted female clothing. At the feast of Hera at Samos, the men wore long, white robes and placed their hair in golden nets. Dionysos was originally a vegetation deity, and in fourth-century Egypt men adopted women's clothes for the procession in his honour. At the Laconian festivals of Artemis (also, originally, a spirit of vegetation and growth) men dressed as women and wore grotesque masks. At

A Kathakali dancer in Ceylon being helped into his costume

indeed, a representation of that ultimate but fruitful Chaos which the myths of androgyny confirm. In Plato's *Symposium*, Aristophanes's quasi-comic speech on the nature of love puts the same point in a less generalized way: 'So ancient is the desire of one another which is implanted in us, reuniting our original nature, seeking to make one of two, and to heal the state of man. Each of us when separated, having one side only, like a flat fish, is but the tally-half of a man, and he is always looking for his other half.' Man is deeply dissatisfied with his own nature, literally torn in half by sexual and generic difference, and through the medium of the transvestitic shaman – or through transvestitic festivals – he aspires toward some original unity.

In this sense, ultimate reality is something which the rational mind does not comprehend; it is a force which cannot really be harnessed by conventional sexual and social distinctions. The folly, the grandeur, the hysteria and even the madness of the shaman are an integral part of his transvestism: his cross-dressing is designed to be irrational, but he resolves through his appearance the arbitrary divisions of ordinary human existence.

But shamanistic transvestism, and its sacred purpose in religious festivities, could survive only as long as the phenomenon itself was feared and respected. When those sacred ties have been unloosed, all that remains is the grotesquerie, the striking disparities which cross-dressing embodies. We may still be deeply afraid of it – transvestism evokes a range of anxieties in many people – but the fear can be dissolved by laughter. And so, as the festivals themselves degenerated, the transvestites became farceurs or used their dressing as a camouflage for sexual excess. The greater freedom of the numinous gave way to the smaller freedoms of the body.

(Opposite, above) *South Indian Bhoota dancers cross-dressing in order to deceive and thus ward off evil spirits*

(Opposite, below) *Kathakali dancers, Ceylon*

festivals in honour of Cotys, or Cottyto, the goddess of sexuality, the men danced in female attire. Such practices, now divested of their original meaning and purpose, are still re-enacted; it was common at European harvest festivals for the last sheaf of corn to be 'dressed up' and, at harvest ceremonies in Bavaria, it is still the custom for the officiating reaper to dress as a woman.

Transvestism, then, acted during these rituals as a preparation for, and sign of, rebirth: to change nature, Man must also change himself. But cross-dressing is, obviously, also a way of lifting all of the established social and sexual constraints. It mocks conventional human values by inverting the elaborate economic and moral sign system which human clothing represents; it becomes, in other words, a radical act with potentially enormous consequences for the individual and society. Mircea Eliade has suggested that transvestitic practices, are

3
TRANSVESTISM REJECTED

One of the major problems in any discussion of transvestism is the fact that it is not a single, unified phenomenon; it exists on many levels, and for many different reasons. Since it is not purely of sexual origin, the deviancy which it represents has been perceived as a threat in various ways. In order to combat it, there have been legal restraints – it was until quite recently in England an offence for a man to wear women's clothes in the street, since he was liable to cause 'a breach of the peace'; there have been religious prohibitions which took their inspiration from Deuteronomy – 'The woman shall not wear that which pertaineth unto a man, neither shall a man put on a woman's garment; for all that do so are abomination unto the Lord thy God' (22:5); and there have been social constraints – transvestites have been considered so powerfully subversive that they have been imprisoned and even executed.

Cross-dressing, however, is not an easy activity to repress; it is so deeply rooted in festive celebration and anarchic display that it survived centuries of persecution. It passed from the pagan rites of antiquity into medieval folk ceremonies and seasonal festivities, the relics of its ancient power attenuated but strong and pervasive enough to emerge in contemporary mumming and pageants. This history is only intermittently visible, since the phenomenon itself was so excoriated and misunderstood that only traces of its progress still remain.

Even though much of its religious symbolism had been forgotten or simply neglected, the anarchic possibilities of cross-dressing were thoroughly explored during the classical festivals of Kalends and Saturnalia. Contemporary reports describe how men dressed as women at these celebratory and initiatory rites and, as Herodotus put it

A transvestite at the New Orleans Mardi Gras

(Opposite) *The Cycle Sluts, an American transvestite group. Overt and outrageous transvestism has become an integral feature of many forms of modern entertainment*

Red-figure cup by Peithinos, fifth century BC, *with transvestite, homosexual scenes*

of the Scythian transvestites, 'Dionysos leads these people on to behave madly.' Indeed, transvestism is an effective and even necessary force on such occasions: it has been characterized as a sheerly pleasurable activity, serving no overtly useful or social purpose, and is well suited to be an emblem for misrule of all kinds.

Its libertarian aspects, together with the incipient paganism involved in cross-dressing, clearly represented a threat to medieval Christianity. The Feast of Fools, for example, was an occasion when both laymen

and clergy dressed as women, howled in the church aisles, and 'farced' the rituals of the Mass. (It was held at the same time as the Feast of Circumcision, and so this farcical cross-dressing is perhaps coincidentally related to early transvestitic rites of initiation.) Alcuin, in the ninth century, writes of men adopting women's clothes at such festivals and 'losing their strength' as a result. At Sens, the priests cross-dressed and sang in falsetto. In 1445, the Faculty of Theology at the University of Paris referred to priests 'who danced in the choir dressed as women'. And so transvestism of this kind bore the brunt of ecclesiastical attacks: towards the end of the fourth century, St Asterius, Bishop of Amasia in Cappadocia, severely criticised those males who on New Year's Day dressed as women 'in long robes, girdles, slippers and enormous wigs'. Bishop Isidore of Seville (560–636) complained of New Year's dancers 'womanising their masculine faces and making female gestures'. Such attacks are not surprising. Transvestism, and the rites associated with it, represented the overt sexuality and the anarchic possibilities of life which Christianity tends to suppress. Indeed, the activity of cross-dressing is in a sense the reverse image of orthodox religion, since it originally derives from ecstatic cults and is pervaded by the notion of the ultimate triumph of Chaos.

When the Feast of Fools was secularized in the sixteenth century, in the festivities associated with the election of the Lord of Misrule, its transvestitic aspects become clearer and better documented. The Lord of Misrule himself, according to Stubbes, chooses 'twenty or sixty or an hundred lustiguts to serve him', who are dressed in female clothing 'borrowed for the moste parte of their pretie Mopsies'. At the Shrovetide festival, Naogeorgus writes in *The Popish Kingdome* (1570):

(Opposite, above) *Mummers at Branston, Lincolnshire, c. 1900. Cross-dressing is a characteristic feature of folk rituals*

(Opposite, below) *Salisbury Hob Nob, with figures in drag*

*Both men and women chaunge their weede, the men
   in maydes aray,*
*And wanton wenches drest as men, doe trauell by
   the way . . .*

The same festive cross-dressing occurred
throughout Europe. In France, the Mere
Folle was dressed as a woman and, according
to Gordon Rattray Taylor, his task was 'to
keep up a running commentary on the sexual
proclivities of his followers'. Anthony
Munday describes, in *The Harleian Mis-
cellany*, certain Roman festivities: 'During
the time of Shrove-tide, there is in Rome
kepte a verie great coyle, which they use to
call Carnevale, which endureth the space of
three or fowre days; the gentlemen will
attyre themselves in diverse formes of
apparell, some like women . . .'. Goethe also
comments on the Roman carnival of a later
date: 'The masks now begin to multiply.
Young men, dressed in the holiday attire of
the women of the lowest classes, exposing an
open breast and an impudent self-
complacency, are the first to be seen . . . we
remember a young man who played excel-
lently the part of a passionate, brawling,
untameable shrew.' In medieval France and
Italy there were even male festive societies,
known as 'Abbeys of Misrule', which were
transvestitic in character.

Cross-dressing clearly represents an important alternative to conventional sexual
and social behaviour; it was a troubling and
yet joyful force which was powerful enough
to survive centuries of social and ecclesiastical reproof. But transvestism had not, in
medieval culture, gone 'underground'. Its
manifestations were incorporated within the
social calendar, and it remained part of the
crude but open sexuality of the period.
Indeed, in all those societies where sexuality
and bodily display are not seen as the
primary instigators of sin and corruption,
transvestism has always found a tangible if
marginal role.

The anarchic possibilities of transvestism
were more threatening when, in the early
modern period, they were transposed to a
political level. Political rebels and the
impoverished lower classes have frequently
cross-dressed for the purposes of riot or
demonstration. In 1630, for example, the
Mere Folle and 'her' troupe attacked royal
tax officers in Dijon; in Beaujolais in the
1770s, male peasants put on women's clothes
and attacked their landlord's surveyors; in
Wiltshire in 1631, bands of peasants, led by
men dressed as women who called themselves
'Lady Skimmington', rioted against the
King's enclosure of their forest lands; in
April 1812, two male weavers in female
clothing – 'General Ludd's wives' – led a
crowd in the destruction of looms and fac-
tories in Stockport; the Welsh riots of the
1830s and 1840s, against turnpike tolls and
other statutory taxes, were led by 'Rebecca'
and other transvestites; the Porteous riots of
1736 in Edinburgh were led by men disguised
as women, and their male leader was known
as 'Madge Wildfire'; in Ireland the Whiteboys, who were active in the 1760s, dressed in
long white frocks 'to restore the ancient
commons and redress other grievances'. In
such cases transvestism has a central,
anarchic purpose in the destruction of the
established social order. But the cross-
dressing involved also evokes memories of a
primeval, communal order which social and
economic hierarchies have exploited and
destroyed. Transvestism becomes, in this
context, a general defiance of an acquisitive
and male-dominated society.

In fact, transvestism is only socially
acceptable when it can be controlled – at
annual festivals, where the licensed anarchy
can be seen as a useful escape valve for
otherwise dangerous tensions, and, of course,
in the form of transvestitic prostitution.
Indeed, prostitution is still the most compre-
hensible and therefore 'suitable' form of
transvestism. Because it is considered to
perform a marginal social function, particularly in those societies where women are
not readily available for sexual purposes, it
has at least been tolerated.

There are records of transvestitic prostitution from earliest times. It may, at first,

*A transvestite carnival participant; detail from
Bruegel the Elder's* Dulle Griet

have been associated with the worship of androgynous deities: at the shrines of Ishtar, the Asiatic Venus, transvestites offered themselves to celebrants as a form of propitiatory lust. But not all prostitutes had so sacred a purpose, and there are many descriptions from travellers and social historians of homosexual prostitutes who 'dress up' in order to solicit trade.

The Pueblo Indians of New Mexico kept a trained male prostitute, called *mujerado* or 'man–woman', in each village. In India, homosexual prostitutes who dressed as women were known as *zunkhas* and, according to one nineteenth-century report, had 'painted tresses and swaying hips, florid gestures and painted lips'. In Japan, male geishas were trained in feminine arts and were known as 'sister-boys'. In China during the Sung dynasty (1127–1279) transvestite prostitutes – who were known as *hsiang ku* or 'mock women' – were organized into guilds. In Egypt, the transvestitic prostitutes were called *El-Ginkeyn*: their bodies were completely depilated, their fingers, lips and toes were daubed with henna, and they wore a blossom behind each ear. A traveller reports the similar appearance of transvestitic prostitutes in nineteenth-century Paris, with 'the curled hair, the painted complexion, the bare neck . . .'. This evidence suggests that such cross-dressing also embodied aspirations which would now be characterized as trans-sexual.

The same pattern of dress and behaviour still exists in the Mediterranean countries of Europe, in South America, Africa, and in North America. There they are, the men–women, squatting outside the urinals of Paris, sitting on small chairs off the streets of Rome, moving around together in crowds in Java, standing alone on the street-corners of London and New York. They are, for the most part, despised by homosexuals, rejected by other transvestites, and used by heterosexuals only when the occasion demands it. They are truly the wretched of the earth.

(Opposite) *Transvestite prostitutes in Bugis Street, Singapore*

The public visibility of transvestitic prostitution has meant, of course, that transvestism itself has often been confused with passive homosexuality or general effeminacy. In the reports of transvestitic activity in the seventeenth, eighteenth and nineteenth centuries no real distinction is drawn between transvestites and male homosexuals. In fact, for all practical purposes, there may have been very little: they had all been driven 'underground' where, in the darkness, everyone looks the same. There was a grand disorder everywhere, as though those who were considered deviant were forced into a frantic but in some ways courageous proximity.

Indeed the abandonment of the convention of men playing female parts on stage, in the seventeenth century, is only one symptom of a vast transition in sexual and social behaviour. When boys or men played as women, cross-dressing was in a sense institutionalized as a medium for self-expression and public display. But by the close of the seventeenth century, transvestism was no longer considered to be an acceptable mode of representation. It was a time, after all, when language itself was stripped of ornamentation and when 'men delivered so many *things* in almost an equal number of *words*'; a culture which enshrined literal representation and the powers of Reason is not one to appreciate cross-dressing in either its festive or sexual aspects. Luxury and ornamentation were in themselves seen as vices which, like ornamental style, could lead to social divisiveness. And so transvestism was repressed; the punishments for those who engaged in it were often harsh – the penalty in England was to be placed in the stocks or dragged through the streets in an open cart and in France, as late as 1760, transvestites could be burned to death.

Cross-dressing was seen as being literally irrational:

> *If thou art a Man, forebear*
> *Thus, this motley Garb to wear;*
> *Do not Reason thus displace*
> *Do not Manhood thus disgrace . . .*

57

Maskers; the man in woman's clothes as a symbol of licence and misrule

(Opposite) *Masked carnival figures from an eighteenth-century engraving*

But one of the consequences of such overt public repression is the need for some kind of private or disguised relief. It is no accident that disguises and masquerades were popular throughout the eighteenth century: in an age of rational despotism, displacement and camouflage became important means of access to what is irrational and anarchic. And as the division between the sexes became more rigid and artificial, sexuality itself was rendered more bizarre and deviant. Dressing up in effeminate clothes – perhaps a sublimation of transvestitic impulses – became fashionable, although luxurious clothing itself was seen as an aspect of unnatural lust. The author of *Satan's Harvest Home* (1749) puts it succinctly: 'I am confident that no age can produce a Thing so preposterous as the present Dress of those Gentlemen who call themselves pretty Fellows . . . Master Molly has nothing to do but slip on his Head Cloaths and he is an errant Woman.' In this climate of opinion, transvestism turned from a celebration into an aberration, an activity full of strange rituals and bizarre obscenities which are in marked contrast to the crude naturalism of its earlier manifestations.

Johann Wilhelm von Archenholz, the German historian, describes an example of such activity in the Bunch of Grapes, an English pub near Clare Market in London, in the 1770s: 'On entering the room the guard found two fellows in women's attire, with muffs and wide shawls and most fashionable turban-like bonnets . . . Their faces were painted and powdered and they were dancing a minuet in the middle of the room . . . it turned out that each member of the club had a woman's name, such as "Lady Golding", "Countess Papillon", and "Miss Fanny".' Although such behaviour has generally been classified as homosexual, it seems to me to be as close to transvestism as it is to homosexuality. Not even the most effeminate homosexuals, for example, behave in the manner which Ivan Bloch describes: 'Another pederasts' club held meetings about 1785 in Clement's Lane near the Strand . . . [men] were caught in the act of nursing and feeding

Woman dressed as a man, smoking a cigar – period of Louis Philippe

some of their suffering "sisters" lying in "childbed"! the new-born babies being represented by big dolls.' The history of European culture is marked by such brief and intermittent glimpses of the repressed and misunderstood, with the lives of those people whom we would now classify as transvestites or trans-sexuals invaded by strange needs and rituals which they themselves were scarcely in a position to understand.

The responses to transvestism in the nineteenth century were similarly uncomprehending. A society which represses sexuality, but welcomes prurience, is not one to welcome transvestism in any form except that of comic or lurid drag. Victorian materialism represented the triumph of bourgeois morality in which 'love' itself was used as a form of male oppression. The two sexes were torn apart in the process, and that great divide was reflected in the dress of the period: women had never looked more graceful and more useless, and men shrank into tight, utilitarian clothing. In this context the male transvestite would seem offensive on every level. His cross-dressing is entirely useless and essentially visual, an expression of pleasure rather than of principle and of sexual play rather than of moral duty. He flouts economic sense and sexual custom – but it was not only perverse of men to dress as women, it was also vulgar; it represented a willed descent in the social order.

Transvestism flourished in the nineteenth century for precisely these reasons, and as a result of overt repression it adopted more fanciful and exotic forms. The records are, as always, sparse but they are eloquent. Transvestism is clearly visible, for example, in one of the most famous nineteenth-century scandals: that of the Vere Street coterie. The affair is narrated in Robert Holloway's *The Phoenix of Sodom* (1813); it is here recorded that Mr Cook took the Swan pub in London's Vere Street, and turned it into a resort for homosexuals. One room 'was called the Chaple, where marriages took place, sometimes between a female grenadier, six feet high, and a petit maître not more than half the altitude of his beloved wife. These marriages were solemnised with all the mockery of bride maids and bride men.' Many of the habitués took on female appellations as well as female dress: '"Kitty Cambric" was a coal-merchant, "Miss Selina" was an errand boy in a police station, "Black-eyed Leonora" was a drummer, "Lady Godiva" a waiter, the "Duchess of Gloucester" a gentleman servant and the "Duchess of Devonshire" a blacksmith.' The police raided one of their meetings, but the cross-dressing was so skilful in at least one case that a 'miscreant escaped the vigilance of the officers and the examining magistrates, and was discharged as a woman'.

This kind of transvestism, related to homosexuality, was not uncommon in nineteenth-century London. *The Sins of the Cities of the Plain* (1881), written by a homosexual prostitute known as 'Jack Saul', reveals the widespread practice of cross-dressing. During the course of his professional life, for example, Saul became a member of the Inslip Club where 'I assumed a charming female costume. Fred acted as a lady's maid, fitted my bust with a pair of faked bubbies, frizzed my hair with curling irons, and fixed me up by adding a profusion of false plaits behind. Then he also dressed himself as a girl . . .'.

Saul also describes a transvestites' ball at Haxells Hotel in the Strand: 'there was nothing to see but a beautiful pair of legs, lovely knicker-bocker drawers, prettily trimmed with the finest lace, also pink stockings and the most fascinating little shoes with silver buckles'. But 'I do not believe there was one real female in the room, for I groped ever so many of them, and always found a nice little cock under their petticoats.' He leaves the ball with the notorious Boulton, also known as 'Stella', and they spend the night in a hotel where they are both mistaken for 'gay ladies'. Boulton seems, on the evidence here, to have been closer than Saul to fetishistic transvestism: '"I love," he said, "to look like a girl, and be thought one."' In the midst of their activities, 'Lady Isabel was announced, and I

Regency fashion, 1829 engraving. Men's clothes have, in certain periods, veered toward the decorative, female mould

(Overleaf) *Special cabaret for women, Montmartre c. 1930. The 'men' here are all women*

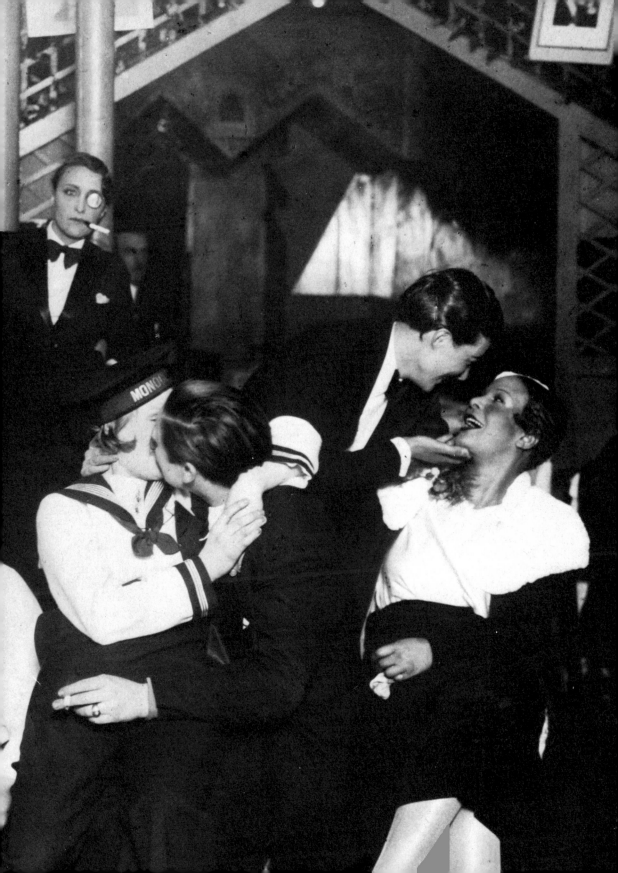

at once recognised Mr Fred Jones.' The cross-dressing recorded here is of an outrageous kind, closer to contemporary drag than transvestism; but, in an oppressive and moralistic society, the deviations in human behaviour become more outlandish and frantic because they are generally compounded by guilt. The exhibitionism of these homosexual transvestites suggests partly the need for sexual excitement, but also a self-induced desire for exposure and punishment.

But cross-dressing, even of this kind, cannot be simply related to homosexuality or to fetishism. This was the way in which it was understood, but implicit in such prurient or horrified accounts are other, unacknowledged factors. The ornamentation and luxury of male cross-dressing were seen as an insult to the economic and moral nature of the male, but the transvestite also breaks down those barriers of 'society' and of class which are themselves based upon social and economic stereotypes. Fred Jones can become Lady Isabel; a blacksmith turns into the Duchess of Devonshire. The mockery of sexual stereotypes involves the mockery of social stereotypes at the same time; when one social code is breached, they are all at risk.

The phenomenon of transvestism is remarkably consistent during this period. Jacobus X records an item from a Berlin newspaper of 1848, entitled 'The Woman-Haters': 'The lady in rose-tarletan that has just now passed by has a lighted cigar in the corner of her mouth and puffs like a trooper. . . '. 'She' is, of course, a man. Jacobus X also records, from nineteenth-century Vienna, the examples of a hairdresser called 'French Laura' and a butcher, known as 'Fanny the female pork-butcher', who 'never miss an opportunity, during the Carnival, of showing themselves disguised as women'. In Paris, in the 1860s, a 'Great Sodomy Company' was uncovered, composed entirely of Napoleon III's soldiery. In the interior of a fashionable house, 'two wardrobes were discovered filled with all kinds of costumes, feminine of course, and, among them, the costumes worn by the Empress Eugénie in ceremonies and official receptions.' When the soldiers dressed up in these clothes, it was known as 'doing the Empress'. At a transvestite ball in Paris in 1864, 'there were at least 150 men, and some of them so well disguised that the landlord of the house was unable to detect their sex'. In fact, one French banker found the excitement too much and 'expired still dressed in a cherry-coloured satin corset and white petticoat'.

Of course, transvestism was by no means unknown in America during the same period. A clergyman called Parkhurst visited the Golden Rule Pleasure Club, on West Third Street in New York: 'The visitors were shown into a basement divided into cubicles in each of which sat a youth with his face painted, the airs of a young girl, a high falsetto voice and a girl's name.' Dr Napheys writes, in the 1880s, that he 'could tell of restaurants [in New York] frequented by men in women's clothes who indulge in indescribable lewdness'. The general impression of such reports is one of secrecy and repression, combined with an almost hysterical exhibitionism.

It was, in fact, only when the condition of transvestism was properly diagnosed and described that transvestites began to 'come out' in undemonstrative ways. Magnus Hirschfeld records in *Sexual Anomalies and Perversions* that, during the First World War, men came before recruitment boards dressed as women. No doubt the majority of them did so in order to escape military service, but some of them seemed to have other motives: 'If I am to become a useful member of society, I must be allowed to be a woman outside my profession. Only then can I serve the State with the selfless loyalty I desire.'

Transvestites were also, under certain circumstances, accepted within the community at this time. One particular case is worth quoting at length, both because it affords an insight into the difference between American and European attitudes toward sexual matters and also because it is one of the earliest contemporary records of hetero-

(Opposite) *A couple dressed in each other's clothes dancing the tango*

Karyl Norman, a drag artist known as 'The Creole Fashion Plate', in his ordinary clothes

sexual transvestism. It is taken from *The Journal* of Lewiston, Maine (1895):

Commander James Robbins, of Coopers Mill in this State, is one of the prominent men of his community, a citizen generally esteemed as a man of integrity and intelligence. Mr Robbins has a brilliant war record . . . if you are on sufficiently intimate terms with him you will find him indulging in his hobby . . . He wears petticoats. He wears a sort of dress about his hips. He always wears a No. 6 shoe with high heels and graceful, slender shape . . . His lingerie is elaborately tucked and ruffled, edged with lace and fashioned to the most approved model of any lady's wardrobe . . . Amazed neighbours, who were not fully aware of the extent of Mr Robbins's hobby, have been obliged to ask for more details when Mrs Robbins has laconically informed them that it is Jim's ironing . . . In the morning he wears print gowns, for he assists in the housework. Almost every morning Mr Robbins in his print gown is seen sweeping off the piazza and whisking about the kitchen . . . One cashmere dress is quite a favourite, and this is worn by Mr Robbins when he promenades in the orchard.

This account is unusual both for its courteously ironic tone, and for the bemused but mild reactions of Mr Robbins's wife and neighbours.

But another case, attested by Magnus Hirschfeld, suggests the more familiar mixture of pathos and theatricality with which transvestism usually invests the individual. In 1903, in Dortmund, 'a young man committed suicide in a hotel where he had arrived the previous day. He was a thirty-two-year-old workman from the district of Koslin in Pomerania. When the door of his room was forced open, he was found stretched out on his bed, dressed in a white bridal gown and veil; on his head was a garland of myrtle. He had shot himself in the heart.' There is no reason to doubt that, during the period we have examined in this chapter, there existed – silent and unrecorded – a large number of transvestites whose lives were as desperate and unrelieved as that of the workman from Pomerania.

(Opposite) *Transvestism often involves an element of unconscious humour*

The Roaring Girle.

OR
Moll Cut-Purse.

As it hath lately beene Acted on the Fortune-stage by
the Prince his Players.

Written by *T. Middleton* and *T. Dekkar*.

My case is alter'd, I must worke for my liuing.

Printed at *London* for *Thomas Archer*, and are to be sold at his
shop in Popes head-pallace, neere the Royall
Exchange. 1611.

4
THE FAMOUS CASES

The recorded instances of individual transvestism are comparatively rare, and even in
the eighteenth and nineteenth centuries the
evidence at our disposal is slim; the available
material has generally to do with carnivals,
political revolts or the eccentricities of
homosexual clubs. But it is interesting to
note that when cases of individual transvestism are described, they generally concern
heterosexual transvestites or latent and
unacknowledged trans-sexuals.

The earliest descriptions of transvestism
are characteristically connected with in-
dividuals who would in any case be unique
and identifiable – the deviations of rulers and
sovereigns are, for example, recorded together with their more public characteristics.
In these cases, cross-dressing was considered
to be no more than a harmless weakness. The
Roman Caesars were reported to show a
fondness for wearing women's clothes and
Caligula, according to Suetonius, often
adopted female clothing. Heliogabalus
entered the gates of Rome in a trailing robe
of silk and gold, with blackened eyebrows,
painted cheeks, and a tiara, demanding to be
honoured as 'empress' by the Romans. There
is some evidence to suggest, however, that
Heliogabalus had trans-sexual rather than
transvestitic impulses since it is reported
that he tried to castrate himself in the
service of a Syrian deity, whom he already
worshipped in female clothing; but, having
been convinced of the imprudence of his
plan, he made do with self-inflicted circumcision.

The behaviour of other monarchs has been
less colourful but no less determined. When
Queen Christina of Sweden abdicated in
1654, she immediately adopted male attire
and for a time went under the name of 'Count
Dohna'. On her well-publicized and controversial peregrinations throughout Europe,

*'Monsieur' – Philippe de Bourbon, Duke of
Orleans, and son of Louis XIII*

(Opposite) *The frontispiece to the Life of Mary
Frith, alias 'Moll Cutpurse', a female transvestite of
the sixteenth century*

69

she wore men's clothes or an uneasy amalgam culled from both sexes. Henry III of France is reported to have dressed as an Amazon, and to have encouraged his courtiers to do the same. A better-attested case is that of Philippe, the brother of Louis XIV, known as 'Monsieur'. Mademoiselle de Motteville writes that 'He loved to be with women and young girls, and attire them and dress their hair.' And Saint-Simon has left a sharp portrait: 'He was a little pot-bellied man, mounted on such high heels that they were more like stilts, always dressed as a woman, covered with rings and bracelets.'

Emil August, Duke of Saxe-Gotha and Altenburg (1772–1822) had similar inclinations. He assumed power in 1804, and

Sardanapalus, the Assyrian king, clothed in female attire, spinning with his wives

was the grandfather of Prince Albert – hence the great-grandfather of King Edward VII. But a less likely ancestor for the British Royal Family can hardly be imagined. As Magnus Hirschfeld puts it, 'All who knew him were struck by his "lady-like" personality. He also wore feminine adornment.' The painter Seidler records that 'he received us lying in bed. During the conversation he rolled the sleeves of his white and capacious night-gown coquettishly up to his shoulders and showed us his arm, which was adorned with a whole row of most magnificent bracelets. A kind of boudoir cap, trimmed with costly lace, covered his head.' Emil August himself records, in a letter to Sidonie von Dieskau, that 'self-love and self-esteem flared up in me and, feeling stronger and better than before, there soon fell from my Ego the pitiful dross, stuck on with such difficulty, of the mannishness forced upon me'. The tone and content here suggest that August's overt transvestism was the expression of transsexual impulses, impulses which had yet to find a name.

But it was not only, or even predominantly, men who became notorious for their cross-dressing. The *Acta sanctorum* inscribes the histories of many women who dressed in the clothes of men in order to become monks or hermits. St Pelagia assumed a male garment of haircloth, and went under the name of *frater Pelagius monachus et eunuch-us*; the cult of the bearded woman saint was part of the medieval folklore of Western Europe, and there is an obvious parallel with the bearded deities of pagan religion. And the apocryphal history of 'Pope Joan', who gave birth to a child during her ostensibly male pontificate, is perhaps a parodic version of the religiosity which came to be associated with female cross-dressing.

In this context Joan of Arc is the most prominent example of female transvestism. The first request that Joan made of the Dauphin was that she be allowed to wear men's clothes, and Marie Delcourt, in *Hermaphrodite*, asserts that transvestism was actually 'the cause of her death'. It certainly formed a vital part of the evidence against her, and for Joan herself male clothes possessed some symbolic importance which she explained in terms of a divine injunction: 'The said Catherine and Margaret [the saints whom Joan saw in vision] commanded this woman to take and wear the dress of a man; and she wore it and still wears it . . .' . There have been suggestions of lesbianism in Joan's adoption of male clothing (female cross-dressing has often been connected, incorrectly, with sexual deviancy), but a woman's transvestism can have different purposes. It can mark, for example, a symbolic break with her conventional feminine

Joan of Arc

71

role: with the demands of possessive male sexuality, and also with the social and familial constraints imposed upon her. The medieval association of transvestism with sorcery emphasises just how explosive and threatening such a 'liberation' might seem.

But kings and saints are only part of our history. There have also been ordinary men and women whose obsessions became so great that they abandoned the clothes of their own sex, often at great risk to themselves, and whose activities seemed at the time so extraordinarily bizarre that they burned their image in the minds of contemporaries.

Mary Frith, known as 'Moll Cutpurse', is one of them. One contemporary said that 'her heroick impudence hath quite undone every *Romance*' and she herself was aware of the ambiguous and farcical aspects of her life: 'let me be layn in my Grave on my Belly . . . and that as I have in my LIFE been preposterous, so I may be in my Death'. She was born in London in 1589 and was, according to *The Life And Death of Mrs Mary Frith*, 'a very towrig and rumpscuttle' from her earliest years. She always had a natural aversion to feminine clothing, and was especially hostile to the 'mincing obscenity' of female behaviour. It became clear quite quickly that 'she was not made for the pleasure or delight of Man' and she decided that 'since she could not be honoured with him she would be honoured by him in that garb and manner of rayment he wore'. And so 'she resolved to usurp and invade the Doublet'.

In male costume she worked with a shoemaker for a while, but eventually decided to 'live by the quick' – as a thief or ruffian. There must have been an element of bravado or despair in this adoption of what is, at the best of times, a precarious existence since Mary Frith herself says, 'I beheld myself more Obnoxious to my Fate, and to have a greater quarrel with that, than the world can have against me.' It is not possible to ascertain whether Mary Frith was a fetishistic transvestite, a lesbian, a latent trans-sexual, or a hermaphrodite (the instruction that she be laid 'on my Belly' in her grave suggests the possibility of the last); it is known only that she cross-dressed, and that she suffered from the same despair which that condition seems to induce, even in our own time: 'It was my Fate not Me; I doe more wonder at myself than others can do . . . when viewing the Manners and Customs of the Age, I see myself so wholly distempered, and so estranged from them, as if I had been born and bred in the Antipodes'. Her alienation was compounded by the indignities which she had to endure: she was once arraigned 'for wearing undecent and manly apparel', but not even public obloquy reconciled her to feminine clothing and those 'Finicall and Modish excesses of attire'.

It is not surprising, then, that she was hounded during the period of the Puritan Commonwealth since in her dress and behaviour she denied all the observances of a repressive society. Indeed, she became known as the 'Queen of Misrule', and her cross-dressing is closely related to the conventional folk-image of the 'unruly woman'. The ambiguity which existed in her own character, at once both assertive and anxious, is one which also existed in the social attitudes towards female cross-dressing. In one sense the female transvestite is both threatening and dangerous – the 'woman out of place' is an emblem of brutal oppression and disorder – but in another sense she adopts the festive role of female unruliness; as Natalie Davis puts it in her remarkable essay in *The Reversible World*, 'The Woman on Top', it is 'to defend the community's interests and standards, and to tell the truth about unjust rule'. But these generalizations, plausible though they sound, do not touch the heart of Mary Frith's life. On her grave is inscribed:

> *Dust to perplex a Sadducee*
> *Whether it rise a HE or SHE*
> *Or two in one, a simple pair*
> *Nature's sport and now her care.*

It was a life of perplexity and sometimes misery for herself, a source of indignation or humour to others.

The Abbé de Choisy wearing his clerical garb in a feminine manner

The activities of the Abbé de Choisy, described at the beginning of this book, were received with less hostility because he lived in a society and amongst a class which considered his cross-dressing to be no more than a harmless diversion. His memoirs (which he describes as 'my comedy') – written when he was in his sixties and seventies – are remarkably revealing. One item of interest is an explanation of his transvestism in terms of infantile experience: 'A habit acquired in infancy is strange, it is almost impossible to overcome: my mother, almost from my birth, accustomed me to women's garments and I continued to wear them in my youth.' It would be misleading, however, to suggest that the *Memoirs* brim over with psychological insight; they tend to be written in a coy and over-elaborate manner which suggests a self-induced blindness toward his own condition. But certain characteristics emerge as if by accident. There is, for example, a distinct element of narcissism: 'I had considered carefully whence came such a bizarre taste, and here is my explanation: the attribute of God is to be loved, adored; Man, as far as the weakness of his nature allows, wishes for the same but, as it is beauty that kindles love and since that is usually the lot of women, when it happens that men have, or believe themselves to have, certain traits of beauty, they try to enhance them by the same methods that women use, which are most becoming. They feel the inexpressible pleasure of being loved.' De Choisy's heterosexuality is never in doubt, but it is accompanied by a kind of fetishism. He always

73

Miss Christina Davies (1667–1739), who served under Marlborough in many campaigns

An eighteenth-century female sailor: Hannah Snell

dwells, in admiring detail, on the shape and texture of his dresses: 'I had a gown of white damask lined with black taffeta . . . a bodice of heavy silver moire which could be seen in its entirety . . .' and so on. And this fetishism is allied, characteristically, with a sense of secrecy and hidden power: 'It is sweet to deceive the eyes of the public.'

It is important to notice here that de Choisy's fetishism was reaching the height of its obsessiveness at exactly that time when male fashions in France came as close as they would ever get to the feminine mode: the men wore lace with profuse ribbons, their periwigs elaborately piled and powdered. This suggests that, contrary to received opinion, transvestism can actually flourish at a time when male and female costumes are very much alike. For the transvestite, clothes are the creations of fetish rather than of fashion and he has very little connection with cycles of taste in such matters. In this sense, the phenomenon of 'unisex' and the undefined sexuality of punk are hardly likely to alter the needs or attitudes of contemporary transvestites.

But, as we have already seen, cross-dressing has by no means been a male preserve. In fact in the seventeenth and eighteenth centuries there are more recorded cases of women who dressed and 'passed' as men. Often such transvestism was seen as a natural and ambitious attempt of women to overcome the conditions of their 'inferior' sex, and many female transvestites became public figures by appearing on stage or travelling round the country. But the cross-dressing of other women was considered unnatural and immoral, and they suffered severe privation in their obsessive pursuit of some interior image of themselves.

Miss Christina Davies was born in 1667, and from her earliest years 'she felt a love for boyish amusements and the pleasure she took in manly occupations'. She was married and had two sons, but on her husband's sudden and inexplicable disappearance from home she went in search of him 'dressed in a suit of her husband's clothes'. The cross-dressing must have afforded her a certain

*Mary Anne Talbot resisting recruitment
by a press-gang*

amount of pleasure or relief, since she stayed in male garments for many years and even enlisted in the army under the name of 'Christopher Welsh'. A similar case is that of Hannah Snell, born in 1723, who was eventually to appear on stage as 'Bill Bobstay the sailor' and who opened a pub in London's dock district known as The Widow in Masquerade. She also dressed as a man in order to enlist, although she had first adopted male clothing in order to search for a missing husband. The similarity of the two stories of female cross-dressing suggests an unacknowledged similarity of origin. Both women took on a dominant male role with which they were familiar; as soon as conventional familial restraints had been lifted, they took advantage of their unusual situations by cross-dressing and in a sense passing as their own husbands.

This female 'manliness' – a condition which would now be seen as simply one of independence but which then required the drastic step of actually posing as a counterfeit male – was common. Mary Anne Talbot, for instance, was better known as James Taylor, a sailor. She was born in 1778, and ran the gamut of juvenile naval occupations as drummer, powder-monkey, cabin-boy and steward. There are in her case hints of lesbian inclinations, and 'she actually made a conquest of the Captain's niece . . . the young lady even went so far as to propose marriage'. On her eventual return to England, Mary Talbot was 'still inclined to masculine propensities', and – despite legal threats – was never able to exorcise herself of the cross-dressing which she had practised for so long: 'I resumed the dress of my own sex, though at times I could not so far forget my sea-faring habits, but frequently dressed myself, and took excursions as a sailor.'

Pag 157

B. Cole sculp.

There are other similarly well-attested cases of female cross-dressing throughout this period: Ann Bonny and Mary Read were early eighteenth-century 'female pirates', whose apparent courage, solidarity and aggressiveness have earned them the status of pioneers of 'Women's Lib' – although, indeed, their transvestism might be more accurately seen as a form of collaboration with a male-dominated and sexist world. Molly Hamilton, whose bizarre life was recorded by Henry Fielding in *The Female Husband* (1746), decided, after a lesbian affair, to 'dress herself in men's cloaths', at various times practising as a male 'doctor of physic' and even going so far as to marry three women. She was discovered on each occasion, and she was finally flogged and imprisoned: 'It is to be hoped that this example,' Fielding writes, 'will be sufficient to deter all others from the commission of such foul and unnatural crime.'

Charlotte Charke, a strolling player who published her biography in 1755, dressed in

Ann Bonny and Mary Read, who were convicted of piracy in 1720

male clothes from her infancy; after being disowned by her family as an 'Alien', she earned her living as a male servant or as a male impersonator on the stage: 'I being of the Bulk and Stature of our modern Fine Gentlemen.' But she was never afforded any good-humoured public recognition as a female 'adventurer' or 'roaring girl' – 'My being in Breeches was alledged to me as a very great Error' – and her life seems to have been one of anxiety and unhappiness. 'I have,' she says at the close of her book, 'throughout the whole Course of my Life, acted in Contradiction to all Points of Regularity . . . There is none in the world MORE FIT THAN MYSELF TO BE LAUGHED AT.'

Charlotte Charke's own account suggests the presence of sexual or fetishistic elements in her dressing up (this may account for the public disapproval), but it is difficult to diagnose the exact nature of her case and that of the others recorded here. It is clear that homosexuality was, for some of them, the predominant motive for their transvestism – it has always been relatively easy for female homosexuals to dress as men without arousing excessive public hostility – but it is by no means a common factor. There are indications of latent trans-sexualism in the cross-dressing of female soldiers and sailors – as though some women were so uneasy with their native sexuality that they would go to extraordinary lengths in order to erase it. Such activities were characteristically seen as ambitious rather than degrading, an attempt to be 'as good as' men. Of course, female transvestism would become unsettling if large numbers of women were engaged in it (hence the persistence of Amazonian myths), but it has generally been treated as a harmless and somehow aesthetically pleasing eccentricity. It is not as threatening as male transvestism, and this unacknowledged sexism is a major element in all forms of 'acceptable' transvestism; female cross-dressing actually enhances the putative superiority of male culture.

Ridicule and incomprehension are, in contrast, the conventional public responses to male transvestism and no one had to endure them more than the Chevalier D'Eon. He is the most famous transvestite in European history, and, as mentioned earlier, has become so closely associated with the phenomenon that Havelock Ellis suggested that cross-dressing be described as 'eonism'. His life is the most extraordinary, his character the most ambiguous, and his public reputation the most controversial of all the transvestites we have encountered.

Charles D'Eon was born in France in 1728, and was dressed by his mother in feminine clothes in his earliest years. He resumed male attire, though, and seems to have lived as a male in his youth and early twenties. But there must have been, at this stage, some suspicion or evidence of his transvestitic impulses. In 1755 he was sent to the court of the Empress Elizabeth at St Petersburg in order to act as a spy, and for that purpose was dressed as a young woman and given the

Ann Mills, another female sailor of the period

name of Madame Lia de Beaumont. This episode in D'Eon's life is one of the few to have been contested but Edna Nixon, in her biographical study *Royal Spy*, describes a portrait of D'Eon completed about this time: 'It shows a pretty young woman wearing a dainty lace cap, drop pearl earrings, a black velvet ribbon round the neck, and a low lacy décolletage revealing a full breast.' The Russian mission was, at all events, something of a success and this early venture into public cross-dressing was to affect the rest of D'Eon's life.

On his return from Russia, he began a military career by commanding a company of dragoons; but his great potential for camouflage and dissimulation must have been recognized, since he was recalled into the French Secret Service and, in 1762, arrived in London as a Minister Plenipotentiary. The history of his next fifteen years is one of controversy and paranoia; from the beginning, D'Eon's extravagant and impetuous behaviour 'gave great umbrage to the Ambassador'. D'Eon was notoriously insecure and aggressive, his anxieties perhaps deriving from the ambiguous reputation concerning his sexuality. He wrote, in later life, to the Comte de Broglie, 'I am extremely mortified at my being what nature has made me, and that the dispassionate nature of my temperament should induce my friends to imagine, and this in Russia, France and England, that I am of the female sex.'

His behaviour, however, became intolerable and the French Ambassador in London complained to Louis XV. The King recalled D'Eon, but the Chevalier refused to leave England and formally broke off relations with his employers. At this point it is reported that he was bribed in order not to reveal to the English those State secrets with which he had been entrusted; certainly, during this period, he was convinced that plans to kidnap or assassinate him were being formulated. It is as if he were inclined to provoke both attention and contumely, in order to complement his own exhibitionism and paranoia.

His relations with the French court certainly became more strained and ambiguous; finally the new king, Louis XVI, sent his envoy, Beaumarchais, to England in order to make peace with D'Eon and to persuade or cajole him back to France. It is here that D'Eon's extraordinary capacity for myth-making became most apparent; he actually persuaded Beaumarchais, who was by no means an unintelligent or unobservant man, that he was indeed a woman, trapped in male clothes in order to serve the State, desperately in need of money to survive.

The news would not have come to Beaumarchais as an absolute surprise, since D'Eon's appearance and behaviour had already aroused a great deal of speculation. Louis Petit de Bachaumont records in his *Memoirs secrets* that 'the rumours which have prevailed for several months concerning the Sieur D'Eon, this fiery personage, so well known for his eccentricities, are to the effect that he is no more than a woman dressed as a man. In England people are so stirred up by these suggestions that the betting for and against amounts to more than a hundred thousand pounds sterling.'

D'Eon was touchy and displeased about his controversial status – he even entered the London Stock Exchange and demanded an apology from those people who were underwriting such an extraordinary amount of money – but it did not prevent him from using it in his encounters with Beaumarchais. In fact, Beaumarchais wrote to the King that 'the positive declaration of her sex, and her promise to live for ever in female attire, will be the only means of putting an end for the future to all kinds of clamour'. D'Eon was now ready to return to France, hoping, no doubt, for financial and social rewards after his long service in England. But one of the conditions for his return stated that 'the phantom of the Chevalier D'Eon entirely disappear and that a public declaration, clear, precise and without ambiguity as to the real sex of C.G.L.A.A.T. D'Eon de Beaumont be made before her return to France and the resumption of female attire'.

Not even this declaration ended the financial speculation in London concerning

The Chevalier D'Eon in female clothing

Caricature of the Chevalier D'Eon

D'Eon's sex. The year of most ambiguity was 1777: within two months, he had appeared both in the uniform of a captain of the French cavalry and also 'dressed in an elegant sack, her headdress adorned with diamonds and bedecked in all the other elegant paraphernalia of her sex'. There is a certain grand insanity about D'Eon during this period, both courting and disliking public attention, despising and exploiting his ambiguous gender.

In any event, he returned to France – towards the end of 1777 – as a woman repentant. But he appears to have been uncomfortable in this new, permanent state of transvestism: 'I try to walk with pointed, high-heeled shoes, but more than once I have nearly broken my neck. Instead of curtseying I have at times taken off my wig . . .'. When he was presented at Court, he gave every sign of awkwardness in female attire. A contemporary account reads that 'the long tail of her dress and the three types of ruffles contrast so ill with the attitudes and quips of a grenadier that the effect is one of low company'.

D'Eon's time in France, constricted and supervised, was not a happy one; he returned to England in 1785, still dressed as a woman, and for a while became an accepted if somewhat eccentric figure in London society. But, as always, he suffered from financial problems and to alleviate the pressure of debt he took up a new career as a female fencer, performing all over the country. This was not an activity, of course, which could continue indefinitely, and the last years of D'Eon's life seem to have been lonely and melancholy. He wrote in his private diaries, 'My life is always the same. I never go out but stay at home, always at work, in bed, or in my room.'

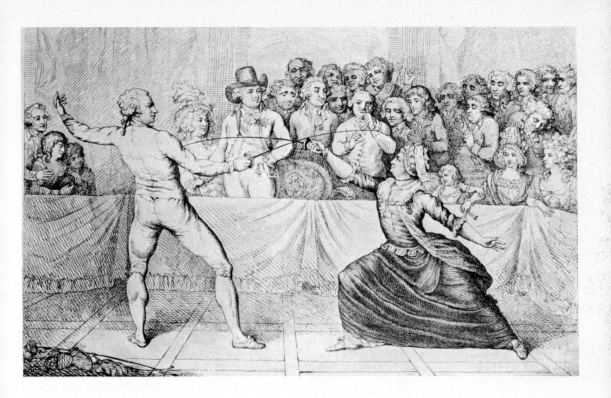

D'Eon as a female fencer

Edna Nixon points out that 'In these entries, written in French and intended presumably only for her eyes, all references to herself are made in the feminine gender.' And yet, on D'Eon's death, the body was laid out – and it was that of a man.

What kind of creature was D'Eon, in turn threatening and paranoiac, vindictive and placatory? He created fantasies out of his sexuality as obsessively as any of his contemporaries, and in fact went to great lengths to preserve the ambiguity of his condition. His is a case of transvestism in which the fetishistic and exhibitionistic traits were developed to a theatrical degree; he could be a petulant male, quick to take insult, and also an aggressive, wise-cracking female – the human being plunged into the deepest disorder which the artificial distinctions between the sexes can create. And so he retreated into a crafty and neurotic secrecy, rejecting the attention which he craved, unsure himself about his true gender.

As M. Cadéac points out in his study of D'Eon, 'the adult mythomaniac is the child prolonged'; it does seem in part that D'Eon's persistent and grandiose transvestism was a retreat into some infantile condition in which reality and fantasy need not be distinguished. His infantilism rendered him both self-consciously voluble and insecure, retreating at any moment into a kind of petulant, asexual introversion, jealously retaining 'power' over other people because of the hidden secret of his sex. The mystery could not, of course, be maintained for ever; but the final revelation of D'Eon's sexual identity has a certain poignancy when we remember his response to the controversy he himself had created, 'Man or woman? I am none the better nor the worse.' The French

'James Barry' with her poodle and black servant

historian Jean de Lacretelle describes D'Eon's life as one 'of much labour and suffering, mixed with very little repose'. But D'Eon should be allowed his own memorial: 'I have been the plaything of Nature . . . I have gone through all the strange vicissitudes of the human condition.'

A similar description could be attached to the life of 'James Barry', a woman who passed as a man for the whole of her life. She also exhibits characteristics remarkably similar to those of D'Eon: petulance, irritability, great intelligence, a kind of neurotic obstinacy and single-mindedness, and what was described as her 'gift of attracting attention'. She was born in 1799 and seems to have lost her female identity immediately; at the age of ten, she was enrolled as a male medical student at Edinburgh University. At the beginning of her thesis, which she completed at the age of twelve, she quoted in Greek some words of Menander – 'Do not consider my youth; but consider whether I show a man's wisdom' – which seem ironically intended from a girl who was to conceal her sex successfully until her death.

Barry enlisted in the army in 1813, and was sent to Cape Town where she became physician to the Governor. At the age of seventeen she acquired a considerable reputation as a physician who, as June Rose puts it in her biography *The Perfect Gentleman*, 'practiced preventive medicine years ahead of her time'. In 1822 'James' became Colonial Medical Officer but her impetuous and overweening behaviour made her few friends; she was shuttled around from one colony to the next – the Windward and Leeward Islands, Corfu, Malta, Canada – provoking arguments and confrontations wherever she went.

Indeed, her character has been described by June Rose as possessing two distinct attributes: 'the passionate termagant, shrilling at authority and making enemies everywhere, and the infinitely generous and patient doctor'. Her cross-dressing allowed her to surpass the conventional distinctions between the sexes, but only at the cost of tearing her nature apart – leaving her exposed, sensitive and vulnerable. It seems to

Boulton and Park being led from Bow Street Police Station to a waiting van

have induced, as it did with the Chevalier, a kind of schizophrenia from which there was no possibility of escape. James Barry died in 1865.

But perhaps the most famous case of transvestism in the nineteenth century is that of Boulton and Park. With them we leave the restless and disturbed world of heterosexual cross-dressing and return to the garish and often unconvincing theatre of homosexual transvestites. Ernest Boulton and Frederick Park – known popularly as 'Stella' and 'Fanny' – were arrested outside the Strand Theatre on 28 April 1870. They were both dressed entirely in women's clothes, and it was in that state that they were brought before the Bow Street magistrates for 'conspiracy to commit a felony'.

At the subsequent trial, Boulton's cross-dressing seems to have come most heavily under attack. Mr John Stafford Fiske, the American Consul at Leith, had written letters to 'my darling Ernie'. 'He tells me you are living in drag. What a wonderful child it is! I have three minds to come to London and see your magnificence with my own eyes.' The letters of a young Edinburgh solicitor were also read out in evidence: 'Even in town I would not go to the Derby with you in drag,' he wrote to Boulton, '. . . I am sorry of your going about in drag so much. I know the moustache has no chance while this kind of

Edward Hyde, Governor of New York and New Jersey (1702–1708), parading the streets in female attire

thing goes on.' And, indeed, the moustache did not. Boulton's mother was called as a witness for the defence and stated that her son 'was twenty-two years old, and had dressed up as a girl from the age of six. As a child his favourite role was that of parlour maid, in which he deceived his own relations.' Her testimony seems to have cast Boulton's cross-dressing in a dramatic rather than sexual light, and both he and Park were eventually acquitted.

Transvestism can, as we have seen, cover a multitude of forms. The cross-dressing of de Choisy and D'Eon was obsessive, cerebral and fetishistic; that of Boulton and Park was

Florence Hensey MD, convicted for treason in 1758

Charles Edward Stuart, known as 'Bonnie Prince Charlie', disguised as a woman

George Sand

outrageous, exhibitionistic and less troubled. And yet the behaviour of 'Stella and Fanny' merited public obloquy and the threat of vengeance. Their appearance explicitly defied the fundamental ethos of their society; by refusing to adopt the phallic and utilitarian model of male clothing, and by asserting instead the primacy of pleasure and ornamentation, they inverted the codes of a society which had created its sexual and social images in the name of economic progress and material acquisition.

The histories of other transvestites are now available to us only in glimpses. Edward Hyde, for example, cross-dressed while he

Una Lady Troubridge and Radclyffe Hall, the author of the lesbian novel The Well of Loneliness

'Colonel Barker', a woman who for many years 'passed' as an officer in the British Army

was Governor of New York and New Jersey (1702–1708). He bore a remarkable resemblance to his cousin, Queen Anne, and was fond of walking through the streets of New York dressed in clothing similar to hers; it is also reported that he dressed as a female courtesan. Jenny de Savalette de Lange, a French transvestite who died in 1858, dressed as a woman throughout his life. No contemporary portraits of him exist, but he is described as being 'tall, thin, and lop-sided, and she leaned on an umbrella. Her features were hard; her look stern and her voice shrill and cracked. She wore a dress that dated from the Empire or Restoration.'

There are other notable instances of cross-dressing: the Chief of Kaiser Wilhelm II's Military Cabinet dressed as a female ballet-dancer at a ball in the Imperial Court, tried to execute a pirouette and died on the spot. Tom Rowlandson was a highwayman, but of an eccentric kind: he used to dress in women's clothes, and demand jewellery from his victims. Joe Lambert, the circus strong man, began his career as 'Tessie, the girl prodigy of the flying trapeze' and performed in this role until he was twenty. Ella Zoyara was a famous equestrienne, until it was discovered that 'she' was a transvestite whose real name was Omar Kingsley. Frances Anderson was billed as the 'World's Champion Billiardist', until she killed herself with a razor and was discovered to be a man.

Such cases could be multiplied over many pages, and it is tempting to dwell upon the sensational aspects of the lives of these men and women while forgetting that they are only the most prominent members of a generally silent and suffering minority. Even those who, like Mary Frith or the Chevalier D'Eon, gained a measure of public acceptance for their 'double nature' were still invaded by doubts and anxieties. It has not been an edifying history, this survey of the men and women who wrecked themselves against the barriers between the sexes.

(Opposite) *Colette in male clothing, at the age of twenty-three*

5
TRANSVESTISM AS PERFORMANCE

Female and male impersonators, whether in
the shape of principal boys or Japanese
onnagata, have played a major part in the
drama of the last four hundred years – and
female impersonation itself derives from a
tradition which can be traced at least as far
back as classical drama. What is it, then,
about the nature of human society that
nurtures and encourages cross-dressing on
stage? It is clearly not just a comic device –
although in modern drama it has more or less
become so – but is, rather, deeply implicated
in the nature of illusion and spectacle.

In Athenian drama, which was originally
performed during the festivals in honour of
Dionysos, all of the female roles were played
by men. And since such drama is derived
from fertility ceremonies – the Dionysiac
dithyrambs are 'birth-songs' which formed
part of the rites of initiation – the role of
transvestism becomes a predictable and
natural one. In Greek tragedy the men wore
female masks, high buskins and richly
decorated clothes, but this feminine
camouflage would not have seemed in the
least unnatural or inauthentic. Feminine
movements and speech were artfully stylized,
designed to be emblematic rather than
mimetic. Dramatic stylization of this kind
could also be employed for the impersonation
of 'low' or shrewish women, and it was this
comic form of cross-dressing which persisted
and which still seems to exercise a peculiar
fascination.

The comic possibilities of transvestism
were extended in Roman drama (the *ludi
romani* originated, also, in harvest festivities), and a vase-painting of the first
century shows Phaedra 'with a wig of red
curls made especially prominent by means of
stuffing and by shoes on high stilts which are
covered by her dress'. The farcical connotation here is clear. The seasonal festi-

*A Roman actor preparing for a play. His female
mask is on the stand to the right, behind which are
folded his dresses*

(Opposite) *A male Japanese Kabuki player*

89

Men in female attire, from an Attic vase of the fifth century BC

(Opposite, above) *Roman actors dressing for a play at the theatre in Pompeii, c. 100* BC

(Opposite, below) *Transvestite actor, from the title-page of the 1615 edition of Thomas Kyd's* Spanish Tragedy

vities of which transvestism was an indispensable element were feasts of liberation, spreading anarchy and levelling the boundaries between the sexes; comedy performs a similar function, since humour is to be found in those situations in which the normal laws of a society are mocked and inverted. And so cross-dressing, which was often used on stage to parody as well as to represent female behaviour, remained a consistent dramatic presence. It spirit lingered in the mimes, pantomimes and seasonal celebrations of the early medieval period – and, indeed, it persists today in the performances of mummers.

Such festive and communal transvestism, representing the common theme of 'The World Upside Down', is a relic of older and more primitive beliefs which the Church could not exorcise. And even when the Church employed dramatic rituals for its own purpose, in the tenth century, boys and men still adopted the clothes of women. In both pageants and liturgical drama, cross-dressing was the convention: a contemporary report states that the boys were 'arrayde like Angells, and others like Vyrgyns'. It is generally assumed that medieval drama has its origins in the dramatization of the Resurrection, and the further connection of transvestism with myths of fertility should not go unrecorded. But, as always, the grotesque and comic uses of cross-dressing existed alongside its more stylized and symbolic elements. Indeed, festive and anarchic components steadily infiltrated liturgical drama, taking their final shape when Latin was replaced by the vernacular in the thirteenth century. Just as the Church authorities were mocked by cross-dressers during the Feast of Fools, so the comic uses of transvestism slowly despiritualized religious drama. Such characters from the Miracle plays as Noah's wife have, in fact, been considered as the ancestors of the modern pantomime 'dame'.

It would be a mistake, however, to see theatrical transvestism as a purely comic and vulgar affair; there was acting as well as impersonation, and the boys who played

Laurence Olivier as Katharina in The Taming of the Shrew

(Opposite) *Sarah Bernhardt as Hamlet*

women must have been serious and graceful performers in order to sustain their roles. Since no actresses were permitted on stage, techniques of acting were developed to encourage the skilful and natural deployment of feminine characteristics. By the middle of the sixteenth century, in fact, women's roles were solid and complex enough to demand quite special skills of speech, gesture and deportment. And the success of such skills in creating and maintaining the illusion can be judged by the astonishing popularity of child actors in the sixteenth century – it can fairly be said that the Boys' Companies dominated the English theatre until about 1580. The boys, unlike the impersonators of the classical stage, did not wear masks but relied instead upon their expressive talents and their clothes for the best dramatic effects. A contemporary writes that 'her maiesties unfledged minions flaunt it in silkes and satiens'; and there is a reference in Henslowe's diaries to stage-props which include 'skirts of white satin laid with white lace (costing 33s and 4d)' and 'skirts of a woman's gown of silver camplet (costing 55s)'.

It is reported that the first Ophelia was played by Nathaniel Field, that Lady Macbeth was played by Alexander Cooke, and that Robert Goffe took on the roles of both Cleopatra and Juliet. The astonishing artifice which must have been involved in these performances, and the dramatic skills which enabled the audience willingly to suspend disbelief, invest Shakespearian drama with an especial ambiguity and power. That drama does in any case test the social and sexual codes which bind human communities together but the presence of theatrical transvestism also gives the plays a festive and anarchic edge, since cross-dressing was still popularly associated with disorderly pageants and seasonal rites.

Of course, transvestitic acting had its vociferous critics; it was seen by some to be both unnatural and subversive. William Prynne, in 1632, put these fears in a primarily sexual context: '. . . this putting on of women's array (especially to act a lascivious,

Actors from the Japanese Noh theatre

amorous, love-sick play upon the stage) must needs be sinful, yea abominable; because it not only excites many adulterous filthy lusts, both in the actors and spectators . . . but likewise instigates them to self-pollution and to that unnatural Sodomitical sin of uncleanness . . .'. And slowly the repressive conscience triumphed. When the Puritans closed down the theatres in 1642, it was only the beginning of a process which was to erase transvestitic performances from the serious

stage and, by so doing, entirely change the nature of the theatrical illusion.

The height of the specifically transvestitic illusion was reached by the Japanese and Chinese theatres, and it is as well to see of what it consisted. The tradition of male cross-dressing on stage, in both of these countries, is a long and consistent one. And here we can trace an old and by now familiar pattern: the drama which employs transvestites has its origins in sacred and festive rituals, and these rituals generally involve the myths of fertility. Japanese Noh drama, for example, derives from *dengaku*, a folk-dance associated with rice planting and harvesting. Chinese Opera, although fixed in its most recent forms only a century ago, has its origin in the song and dance patterns of ancient Chinese religious festivities.

In these operatic performances, the female impersonators, the *tan*, follow prescribed and highly stylized techniques for the enactment of female roles. A number of fixed gestures are used, and the impersonator wears a female mask corresponding to the kind of woman he is portraying: *chingyi*, an elegant lady, *huatan*, a lower-class woman, or *taomatan*, an Amazon or militant. The performer here is, as Leonard Pronko asserts in *Theater East and West*, 'the master of a complex and extremely rarefied art', an art of images and symbols that denies naturalistic conditions and, therefore, the limitations of native sexuality.

Similarly artificial performances are at the centre of Japanese Noh drama. Again, the plays move slowly and are infused with an intense refinement and spirituality, the 'female' actors wearing masks and following stylized routines throughout their performance. The theatre represents a self-enclosed and spiritual world and, indeed, it might be said that dramatic cross-dressing is a colourful symbol of the androgyny within Buddhism itself which, as Lévi-Strauss explains in *Tristes tropiques*, 'expresses a placid femininity which seems to have been freed from the battle of the sexes, a femininity which is also suggested by the temple priests whose shaven heads make them indistinguishable from the nuns, with whom they form a kind of third sex . . .'.

Since the concept of androgyny is incorporated within the established religion, the presence of men dressing as women – both on stage and off – is not considered as either a moral or social threat. This is perhaps why the tradition of female impersonation has been most successful, and most pervasive, in Japan. Certainly in the other major form of Japanese theatre, Kabuki, the males are expected to perform the roles of women. Kabuki is a later form than Noh, more popular and less ritualistic. But the female impersonators, the *onnagata*, are no less elaborate in their appearance and in their performance. The careful make-up, the stylized gestures and the falsetto voice are designed to reproduce the essence of femininity, with such success that women themselves watch the performances of the *onnagata* in order to learn how to act and react. Leonard Pronko describes one *onnagata* as exhibiting 'a steel-like power hidden by softness . . . with many layers of heavy kimono and a wig weighing as much as thirty pounds'. In this transformation from man to woman, a new being emerges as a strange amalgam of both sexes. The *onnagata*'s power goes beyond his performance, and touches upon the audience's aversion to nature and longing for illusion. The representation of life as it is implies the presence of death; transvestism implicitly defies the necessity of such natural laws by its explicit reversal of natural sexual characteristics.

It is possible that this sense of theatrical illusion, anti-natural and essentially irrational, was present within the English tradition of serious female impersonation. And it may be that its unacknowledged potency accounts in part for the closing of the theatres during the Puritan Commonwealth. Certainly everything changes as a result of that suppression and, after the Restoration and the reopening of the theatres in 1660, another drama emerged.

Sir William Davenant's patent, allowing him to stage plays in public, states that 'whereas the women's parts have hitherto been made by men, at which some have taken offence, we do give leave that for the time to come all women's parts be acted by women'. This dispensation signals the birth of the actress, and the decline of the serious female impersonator. There had been cases of women appearing on stage before – French actresses had performed in England in 1629 but they had been unfavourably received, and Mrs Coleman is said to have played Ianthe in Davenant's 'opera' of 1656 – but this year marks the clear point of change. When Margaret Hughes took the part of Desdemona in 1660, the prologue goes:

Edward Kynaston, the seventeenth-century transvestitic actor, as a boy

The emphasis on 'civilize' is revealing here; it had by now come to be considered uncivilized, literally anti-social and irrational, for men to dress as women. In an age of literal representation, and at a time of male-dominated commercialism, cross-dressing seemed a peculiarly alien and threatening activity. It was fit only to be laughed at – which is, of course, exactly what happened.

For some years female impersonators still worked alongside actresses on stage. Pepys saw women players for the first time in *The Beggar's Bush* of 1661; four days later, he saw Edward Kynaston playing the title-role in Ben Jonson's *The Silent Woman*, with 'the loveliest legs that ever I saw in my life'. Kynaston has some claim, in fact, to being the last serious transvestitic actor in England; highly acclaimed for his skill in impersonating women, he grew into a respectable veteran and 'developed a kind of stately grace'. But he was exceptional; as actresses like Mrs Barry, Mrs Bracegirdle and Mrs Rodgers became more popular, their male counterparts faded into obscurity.

The appetite for sexual reversals on stage, however, did not entirely disappear; soon after actresses appeared in the theatre, they started adopting the roles of men as well. The 'roaring girl', the actress in breeches, became something of a craze in the eighteenth century. But social propriety was not offended by such female aspirations toward manhood; breeches parts became – and remain – a respectable and conventional element in the theatre.

Male cross-dressers were not so fortunate; there were no companies to educate them in what had once been a subtle and skilful art; proper roles could no longer be written for them. When the style and the credibility of the illusion vanished, female impersonators ceased to be actors and became, like Tate Wilkinson or James 'Nursery' Nokes, comics instead. The audience now understood that it

(Opposite) French actors from the Théâtre des Variétés. An eighteenth-century engraving

96

was a man only pretending to be a woman, and the performers began to burlesque themselves. And so transvestism on stage became a comic routine, and its farcical connotations connect it more to the contemporary 'dame' tradition than to anything more subtle or more serious. It is a connotation, in fact, which female impersonation has never been able to lose. Transvestism had lost its sacred function in classical times; it had lost its dramatic authority by the seventeenth century; it was now either suppressed altogether or turned into a comic diversion.

In one instance only did transvestism continue to be accepted as a natural element in the theatre. In the artificial form of Italian opera, developed in the early seventeenth century, the female dresses and the soprano tones of the castrati served to heighten the air of illusion and of fabrication. The castrati often dominated such performances, their style and skill – very different from the theatrical impersonation of the period – bringing them close to the dedication and the artfulness of the Japanese *onnagata*. De Brosses praised Porporino for being 'as graceful as the most graceful young lady', and Goethe describes the skill of the castrati in what have now become familiar terms: 'Thus a double pleasure is given in that these persons are not women but only represent women. The young men have studied the properties of the sex in its being and behaviour; they know them thoroughly and reproduce them like an artist; they represent, not themselves, but a nature absolutely foreign to them.' It is this ability to evoke what is alien, either in appearance or in behaviour, which marks the distinctive talent of the serious transvestitic performer.

When cross-dressing ceases to be stylized, preserving a cool arena of illusion between performance and artist, only the grotesquerie remains. Even in Italy, where no actresses were permitted on stage until 1789, female impersonators exhibited the same signs of artistic degeneracy as their contemporaries in England and France. Johann Wilhelm von Archenholz records in the latter half of the eighteenth century that 'pitiful jack-puddings are acting comedies. When these are disguised, and pretend to imitate the gestures of the fair sex, with their beards and rough voices, nothing can be imagined more ridiculous.' And William Beckford, visiting Portugal in 1787, noticed 'a stout shepherdess in virgin white . . . clutching a nosegay in a fist that would almost have knocked down Goliath, and a train of milk-maids attending her enormous footsteps'. And so the actors who played women's roles, whether serious or comic, were gradually banished to the dramatic 'underground': to fair-grounds, for example, and to groups of strolling players.

When cross-dressing was given space within the established theatre, it was simply to provide comic diversion; when Gay's *Beggar's Opera* was performed in 1781 with all its sexual roles reversed, the *St James Chronicle* described the 'Entertainment, arising from so ludicrous an Inversion'. During the eighteenth and much of the nineteenth century, in fact, the comic effects of transvestism were most extensively employed in pantomime. The harlequinade and its derivatives provide an apt example of the persistence and popularity of cross-dressing. Originally adapted from the *commedia dell'arte*, in which the girl was sometimes disguised as a boy and a man adopted the role of the grotesque female, the English pantomime derived much of its spirit from native traditions of farce and satire – both of them providing a context in which cross-dressing was already a popular device.

The record of specifically pantomimic cross-dressing can be traced back to 1702, in a performance of the Mard Brothers called 'Night Piece': 'What ridiculous Postures and Grimaces . . . and seeming in Labour with a Monstrous Birth, at last my counterfeit Male Lady is delivered of her two Puppets, Harlequin and Scaramouch.' A contemporary account of a later harlequinade suggests another kind of transvestism: 'Grimaldi wears a curious habit surmounted by a large hat bordered with fur, as a satire on the present mode of female fashion.' And, as a suggestion of what was to come, Jefferini

Charles Bannister as Polly in the 1781 production
of The Beggar's Opera

played one of the Ugly Sisters in an 1841 production of *Cinderella* at Sadler's Wells.

The Ugly Sisters were, in fact, to become stock characters on the English stage. And it was in the nineteenth century, disinclined though it was toward the kind of camouflage and alienation which transvestism represented, that female impersonation took on its most grotesque but acceptable face: that of the 'dame'. Burlesqued transvestism was, as we have seen, a regular part of the comic business of the nineteenth-century stage; but with the emergence of the tavern music halls, and then the music hall proper, it found its natural home. E.W. Marshall was 'dressing up' at the Canterbury in the 1850s and, by the 1860s and 1870s, most male and female performers had a 'drag' number in their repertory. Female 'breeches' parts, in acts like those of Vesta Tilley, flourished and during this period female impersonators steadily broadened their roles. It became the routine of impersonators that they would work the halls during the year, and then take on the role of dame in the Christmas pantomime.

And so, by the middle of the nineteenth century, the impersonator in harlequinade had given way to what is still the most popular and extensive form of comic cross-dressing: the pantomime dame exploits a potential which had first been explored in the shrewish wives of the Miracle plays, and which has never ceased to amuse and fascinate English audiences. It has also been suggested that the dame is a survival from the time when elderly female parts were played by men because young actresses were understandably reluctant to age themselves prematurely. There have been many famous dames – George Robey, Wilkie Bard, Malcolm Scott ('The Woman Who Knows') – but arguably the greatest of them was Dan Leno. Max Beerbohm's evocation of his stage presence is remarkable: '. . . that air of wild determination, squirming in every limb with some deep grievance that must be outpoured . . . that poor little battered personage, so put upon and yet so plucky, with his squeaking voice and sweeping gestures; bent but not

Dan Leno in drag

(Opposite) *George Robey, the English comic, as the 'Queen of Hearts'*

101

Madame Vestris as Don Felix

(Opposite) *Robert Helpmann and Frederick Ashton as the Ugly Sisters, 1965*

broken; faint but pursuing'. The expert impersonator, even in comedy, does not simply parody or mimic women; A. E. Wilson, in *Christmas Pantomime*, has recorded that Leno's 'insight into the manners and customs of the working class was acute, and his acquaintance with their vocabulary extensive and peculiar'. The male impersonator, the actress in trousers, seems in contrast to lack depth and resonance. It is, of course, a popular tradition – Madame Vestris has some claim to being the first principal boy, starting a line that stretches into our own time – but the male impersonator is never anything more than what she pretends to be: a feminine, noble mind in a boy's body. It is a peculiarly sentimental and therefore harmless reversal. The female impersonator, on the other hand, has more dramatic presence – the idea of a male mind and body underneath a female costume evokes memories and fears to which laughter is perhaps the best reaction.

That is why the art of the pantomime dame is often so striking. Cyril Fletcher, a contemporary dame, has described it in *Nova* magazine as 'creating a world of complete fantasy, a world of very subtle sexual balances, quite as unsettling and provoking as anything in *As You Like It*'. The dame is never effeminate; she is never merely a drag artist, since she always retains her male identity. The performer is clearly a man dressed as an absurd and ugly woman, and much of the comedy is derived from the fact that he is burlesquing himself as a male actor. And, just as the nature of the performance seems hardly to have changed over the last century, so the dialogue still follows a familiar but comic pattern. In 1937, the dame was saying: 'See who's there; it may be a man.' And, in the sixties, the Ugly Sisters engage in a continual sexual banter: 'It may be vanity but I can sit in front of a mirror for hours looking at my beautiful face.' 'That's not vanity, that's imagination, dear.' Such acts are, characteristically, harmless ways of breaking certain sexual taboos. They evoke, for example, fears of feminine aggression and overt sexuality at the same time as they play

Richard Hearne as Mother Goose, 1954

upon anxieties about male homosexuality; all of these fears are subtly represented, and then detonated. Thus transvestism can be a way of releasing sexual anxieties through laughter.

Although broadly comic transvestism continued in all-male revues and in the acts designed for working men's clubs, a flashier and more outrageous cross-dressing developed in the years between the two world wars. It embodied a novel notion which Roger Baker, in *Drag*, has perceptively described as 'intentional glamour'. In France

(Opposite) *A pantomime dame prepares, 1941*

Female cabaret artistes in Paris in the twenties

Barbette as both man and woman

and Germany, acts of this kind are often performed by trans-sexuals or by overtly fetishistic transvestites. The case of the French entertainer Coccinelle, alias Jacques Dufresnoy, is pertinent here since his female act is more studied than comic, a meticulous illusion which gives very little away: 'I extended my repertoire and changed my appearance each year, trying to base myself on a different type of woman . . . I thoroughly enjoyed admiring myself. I felt at ease, enraptured . . . there was no doubt at all that, as a travesti, I was freed from all my complexes'. The fact that many European artistes, performing in much the same manner as Coccinelle, take hormone pills suggests that their feminine illusion has been powerfully internalized; and that many female impersonators are closer to a kind of latent or explicit trans-sexualism than they are to the comic tradition of dressing up.

They are, in fact, very far removed from the drag act of a contemporary English performer like Danny La Rue. His act is designedly and purely comic – and the comedy is derived from the fact that there is never any doubt that he is a man dressed up as a woman. The illusion of femininity is carefully maintained – Danny La Rue's act is admired by other performers for its meticulous consistency and attention to detail – but he willingly and overtly breaks the spell at the end. The man re-emerges, and so the cross-dressing seems neither aberrant nor threatening; it is all done 'just for fun'. Mr La Rue is clearly not trying to emulate the profoundly comic effects of Dan Leno's impersonations, but he has taken glamorous drag to its ultimate and most comic conclusion.

He has, in this sense, very little to do with the explicitly homosexual drag of pubs and clubs, although the vulgarity and outrageousness of such acts associate them with the early portrayal of 'low' women on the music hall stage. But there is a strong misogynistic element involved in such routines, as though the homosexual rejection of women were somehow magnified – and therefore justified – by the unreal, oversized and over-sexed version of the female:

Coccinelle, the male cabaret artiste

Lindsay Kemp (on the right) and friend

(Opposite) *Andrew Logan, dressed up, with a mustachioed female*

(Overleaf)
Danny La Rue performing a number with Twiggy

Pudgy Roberts, a drag artist

Julian Eltinge

One of the last highly successful stage stars to enter motion pictures. His three pictures by the Lasky-Paramount have been such a sensational success that he is now classed with Fairbanks and Pickford as a drawing card.

Needless to say he will remain in pictures

A poster celebrating the abilities of Julian Eltinge, the American entertainer

'Have a good look dear,' the drag artist Marc Fleming tells his audience, 'it's the nearest thing you'll see tonight to a butcher's window.' Remarks and jokes at women's expense are a constant feature of these performances, as though the image and nature of women need only to be invoked in order to be laughed into oblivion.

Dramatic and comic transvestism has been just as powerful and popular a force in America as in Europe. Indeed, the tradition of female impersonation stretches back into nineteenth-century America, in burlesque and vaudeville, and perhaps the greatest female impersonator of this century was a Bostonian, Julian Eltinge. He was born as William Dalton in 1882, and from the beginning of his career seems to have dressed up in order to play the heroine. Originally billed as 'Miss Simplicity', he toured in vaudeville and made his Broadway debut in 1903. Although his shows, like *The Fascinating Widow* and *The Crinoline Girl*, and his subsequent films were broadly comic, his own impersonations seem to have been of a generally elaborate and meticulous kind. He specialized in 'extraordinary transformations', and his skill at portraying beautiful women – without parodying them – was such that he became the first, and possibly the last, internationally famous transvestitic performer.

There has been a wide range of female impersonators in the United States, their popularity perhaps an emblem of an extraordinarily fluid and sexually ambiguous society. Impersonation of this kind may, in fact, be the sexual equivalent of 'blacking up' by white entertainers in vaudeville – a way of expressing and thus releasing the tensions within a rapidly emerging culture. Certainly cross-dressing was a widespread phenomenon from the earliest years. In the 1900s, Karyl Norman was known as 'The Creole Fashion Plate' (his dresser was, incidentally, his mother); Bert Swor and Francis Renault acquired considerable reputations as female mimics; and, in the twenties, Savoy and Brennan were a popular drag act. Brennan played the 'wench' or 'dumb Dora' while

The Senior Class at Teachers College, New York,
all female

The Gasperone Group, drag in New York at the
turn of the century

Holly Woodlawn in Scarecrow in a Garden of Cucumbers

Savoy dressed as 'the red-haired harlot', characteristically burlesquing the fashions and styles of the period. There was something uniquely American about the sharpness and relaxed obscenity of such acts; Edmund Wilson wrote of Savoy that 'one felt oneself in the presence of the vast vulgarity of New York incarnate and made heroic'.

That 'heroic' tradition continues in the work of American impersonators like Charles Pierce, whose act combines dramatic skill and intense vulgarity in equal proportions; but female impersonators have also adopted less conventional and more contemporary forms. Performers like Holly Woodlawn and Candy Darling tread the boundaries between transvestism and transsexualism, and their extravagant but stylish role-playing differs radically from the acts of other impersonators. Their cross-dressing does not in any way burlesque itself with stagy 'routines'; it does not offer itself as a comic or grotesque spectacle, but rather presents itself as natural and normal. One of the New York Dolls, a transvestitic group, has said that 'I'm not impersonating anybody. I'm perfectly satisfied with what I am.' It is this pleasurable satisfaction in cross-dressing, its projection as a natural and spontaneous human activity, that makes these performers so unusual. They work with such élan and wit that their cross-dressing is both stunningly watchable and radically subversive.

And so there are contemporary American playwrights and directors who have been using transvestism in order to elicit both its theatrical and political symbolism. John Vacarro's Theatre of the Ridiculous arranges quasi-surrealistic extravaganzas like *Bluebeard's Castle*, in which extensive and bizarre cross-dressing becomes a way of deforming the ordinary theatrical illusion. A similar spirit animated one of the most successful French transvestitic groups, La Grande Eugène. The members of this troupe often mimed to music in the conventional manner of the drag artist, but they also recreated themselves in the image of contemporary figures like Angela Davis. Francis Wyndham has written of the group's central figure, Claude Dessy-Dreyfus known as 'Erna von Scratch', that, 'like all great clowns he can pass in an instant from the most enormous laugh to a sort of sacred terror . . . these representations of a reconstituted

(Opposite) *The New York Dolls, rock entertainers*

(Overleaf) *Les Ballets Trokadero de Monte Carlo, an American group of male ballerinas*

Mick Jagger.

And Mick Jagger.

James Fox.

And James Fox.

See them all in a film about fantasy. And reality. Vice. And versa.

performance.

Poster for Nicholas Roeg's film Performance *(1967)*

world reverse and invert the most deeply rooted values and criteria'. The contemporary awareness of precisely these values within dramatic and comic transvestism, values which have been camouflaged or suppressed since the seventeenth century, has now made it possible for cross-dressing to become an integral part of many different kinds of performance.

It has, for example, invaded the ballet – in the shape of Les Ballets Trokadero de Monte Carlo. This American group, founded in 1974, has been described as a 'weapon of sexual politics' but, as one male dancer put it, 'we are not imitating women . . . we are ballerinas'. In all those activities where sexual stereotypes have previously determined the nature of the performance, the invasive power of cross-dressing can become an instrument of change. By inverting or destroying the conventional sexual and public roles, while neither gratifying nor titillating the spectators with familiar humour, transvestitic performers can revolutionize the nature of the dramatic illusion. They cease to be female impersonators, and become an image of artistic freedom. Other activities can also be affected by such explicit sexual reversals: Urs Lüthi is, for example, a 'performance artist' but one whose performance is systematically called into question. He turns his own image into a public spectacle, perpetually rearranging himself in male or female guises. In the

(Opposite) Urs Lüthi, the Swiss performance artist

118

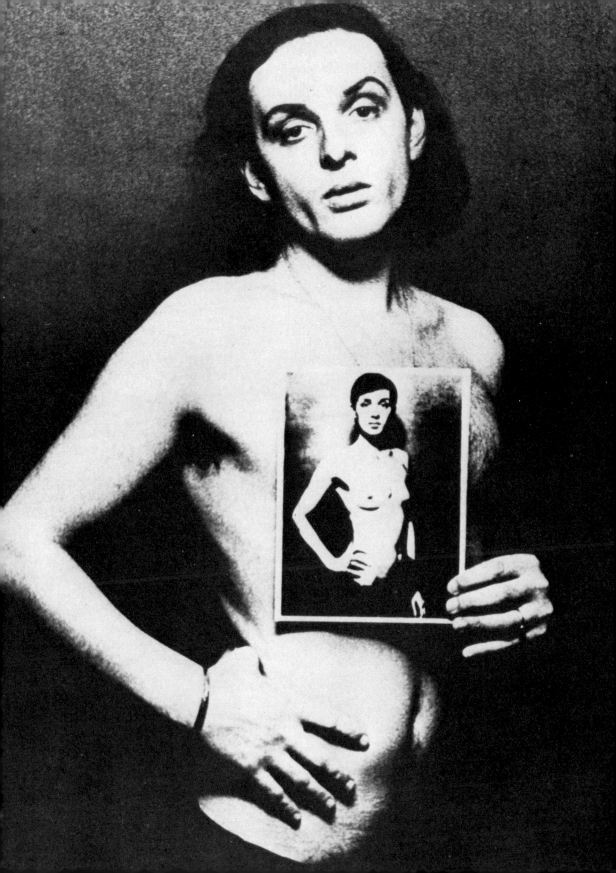

Brian Eno

process, everything becomes deformed or problematical: in a performance where the sexual identity of the performer is not securely rooted, all other social and aesthetic images take on a curiously hallucinatory quality.

That is why transvestism has become a pervasive presence in rock culture, as an emblem of joyful disorder. Alice Cooper, Mick Jagger, and David Bowie's 'gender-fuck dressing' all use cross-dressing as part of their act. It suggests a defiance of the established sexual order on a theatrically convincing scale, but it can also represent those infantile and fetishistic longings which have become a noticeable part of contemporary culture. Auto-eroticism, narcissism and the

(Opposite) *David Bowie*

120

Bob Hope in The Princess and the Pirate *(1944)*

'acting out' of private fantasies play as large a part in rock culture as they do in certain kinds of male transvestism; and if, as one observer has put it, rock music tries 'to make a revolution out of sheer pleasure', we are getting close to Dr Robert Stoller's description of transvestism as 'sheerly pleasurable'. Transvestism can become an infantile and anarchistic force which breaks through the boundaries of repressive civilization. The multi-sexual extravaganzas of the sixties and seventies speak the same message as that of the transvestite: we wish to be what we can make of ourselves. And it may be that, as a consequence, the motives for 'dressing up' will change and that it will become an external rather than an internal event – a performance rather than an obsession. Its period as a fetish and a classifiable 'deviation' may be drawing to a close – at least in the West – and it may revert to its earlier role as a joyful and anarchic force.

The cinema, too, has employed an extensive range of cross-dressing: from the character actor's meticulous imitation of women in certain roles (Laurence Olivier and Alec Guinness have both dressed up with great effect) to the more flamboyant cross-dressing of comedians like Fatty Arbuckle and Mickey Rooney. The spirit of the music hall lingered on in comic drag like that of Charlie Chaplin in *A Woman*, and from the time of the silent cinema there has been a consistent tradition of male and female impersonation. Male impersonators have naturally been considered less bizarre and less threatening, and actresses like Greta Garbo or Marlene Dietrich have made cross-dressing an integral element of their film image. Most of the major American comedians – Groucho Marx, Buster Keaton, Bob Hope – have adopted women's clothes for comic purposes. But perhaps the most elaborate use of drag as a filmic device was *Some Like It Hot*, in which Jack Lemmon and Tony Curtis dress up as a form of disguise; it was this film that prompted Parker Tyler, in *Screening The Sexes*, to record that 'the United States harbours the headquarters of heterosexual female impersonation'.

(Opposite) *Alec Guinness in* Wise Child

(Above) *Mickey Rooney as Carmen Miranda in* Babes on Broadway *(1941)*

(Left) *Charlie Chaplin, in drag, from* A Woman *(1915)*

(Opposite) *Tony Curtis and Jack Lemmon on the set of* Some Like It Hot *(1959)*

(Above) *Buster Keaton, dressed up, in* Doughboys *(1930)*

(Right, above) *Marlene Dietrich, in characteristic male guise, from* Morocco *(1930)*

(Right, below) *William Powell in* Love Crazy *(1941)*

(Opposite) *Cabaret artiste from Visconti's* The Damned *(1969)*

(Overleaf) *Jerry Lewis in a frock, from* At War with the Army *(1951)*

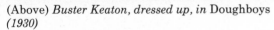

(Above) *Mary Pickford in* The Poor Little Rich Girl *(1917)*

(Left) *Billy House in* Merry Go Round of 1938

Drag has characteristically been used in the cinema for similar kinds of disguise and evasion – this is, after all, the most rational, easiest and least threatening form which it can take. But in the contemporary cinema transvestism has served other than purely comic purposes. It has been employed as a symptom of incest and psychosis in Alfred Hitchcock's *Psycho*, where Anthony Perkins dresses in the clothes of his dead mother; in *Performance* Mick Jagger turns transvestism into an intense and sinister force; and it becomes a narcissistic and quasi-homosexual activity in Visconti's *The Damned* and Jack Smith's *Flaming Creatures*. Indeed, the cinema reflects transvestism in most of its contemporary aspects; the conventional comic potential of 'dressing up' has often been ignored for the sake of more powerful and ambiguous statements about the nature of human sexuality.

(Opposite) *Wally Brown and Alan Carney in* Genius at Work *(1945)*

Roman Polanski, after a suicide jump, in The Tenant

(Opposite, above) *A transvestite male, from* Pink Narcissus *(1971)*

(Opposite, below) *John Crawford in* The Impersonator *(1962)*

But this is merely a description of what is already known, and it is perhaps more interesting to speculate about the reasons for the persistence and popularity of cross-dressing as a dramatic, artistic and cinematic phenomenon. What, specifically, is the public allure of men dressed in women's clothes? Such performances clearly bear the traces of their original anarchic and festive role: the comedy of transvestitic acts is part of a vicarious pleasure in seeing the sexual and social worlds literally inverted. But it has also been suggested that men who perform as symbolic women in some way compensate the males in the audience for the loss or the suppression of their female component; and cross-dressing may, as we have seen, satisfy the persistent wish for anti-nature and the complete, asexual illusion.

133

Augustine Thomas and Otto Flake in a collage by
Louise Ernst-Strauss, 1920

(Right) Picabia dancing, from Entr'acte *(1924)*

(Opposite) *Picasso, in female mask, with Clive Bell.*
Mougins, c. 1939

134

(Opposite) *Stanley Baxter, the Scottish comedian, as an old woman*

Dick Emery as a 'wily old duchess' in his 1977 Christmas Show for the BBC

Hinge and Bracket, alias George Logan (left) *and Patrick Fyffe*

(Opposite) *Barry Humphries, the Australian writer and character actor, in the role of his famous creation Dame Edna Everage*

It would be unwise, however, to ignore the exhibitionistic and fetishistic elements in any analysis of dramatic transvestism. Cross-dressing is often a symbol of infantile sexuality, one of the signs of arrested sexual development, and it is quite natural that a sexuality devoted to illusion and fantasy should find a place in the theatre – in the same way that 'camp' is a theatrical version of male homosexuality. This manner of giving colourfully explicit and dramatic form to some of our deepest and most subversive instincts is one of the most significant aspects of the theatrical illusion. And so it is that transvestism has played, and will continue to play, a major element in dramatic entertainment of all kinds.

'On Dieppe Beach', drawing by Aubrey Beardsley

6
TRANSVESTISM IN LITERATURE

Transvestism, whether male or female, has played a major role in creative literature only in a dramatic context. In prose narratives, especially of a naturalistic sort, the subject has characteristically been too complex or too disturbing to present. When it has emerged, though, the results are often intriguing – and although any compilation of such material is inevitably selective, certain broad themes can be discerned.

The most natural and most rational way of dealing with cross-dressing has been to describe it in terms of concealment or disguise. Men dress themselves as women in order to sneak behind enemy lines or, as in Fenimore Cooper's *The Spy* (1821), to protect themselves from their enemies. In Cooper's novel the central character, Harvey Bank, dresses up as a washer-woman to escape from capture during the War of American Independence; the book concerns itself with disguise and masquerade, and with the confusion implicit in divided loyalties. In such a context, transvestism becomes a potent symbol of ambiguity.

This ambiguity, this crossing of boundaries, can be of most effective use in a romantic or sexual situation. Imaginative literature abounds with instances of men and women who cross-dress in order to be near each other. In *The Greek Anthology*, Paulus Silentarius describes one such lover:

> In her shift he resembled
> Achilles, when he sought
> Concealment midst the women
> At Lycomedes' court.

In D'Urfé's *L'Astrée* (1614–1620), Céladon dresses himself up as 'Orithée' in order to reach his beloved: 'Now it happened that this Youth (without consideration of the great danger) that day attired himself like a sheperdesse, and forcing himself into our

company was taken for a maide . . .'. The innocence and playfulness of such accounts suggest that transvestism was not in itself considered a bizarre or threatening phenomenon; perhaps because of its persistence on the stage, it was considered a form of disguise without any of its contemporary sexual or fetishistic connotations.

The other common literary association of transvestism has been with homosexuality. Juvenal describes cross-dressing in the process of a homosexual 'marriage' and Martial writes that 'bearded Callistratus as a bride wedded the brawny Afer in the usual form as when a virgin weds a husband. The torches shone before him, and a wedding veil disguised his face'. A similar identification is made with homosexual prostitution. In 1886 the pseudo-Byron, in *Don Leon*, writes of a male prostitute:

> I sought the brothel where, in maiden guise,
> The black-eyed boy his trade unblushing plies.

In all these instances, though, transvestism is incidental to the main theme; it has become a kind of embellishment, easily and discreetly handled as a rhetorical device. The heart of the matter is not approached.

Even in the autobiographies and memoirs of cross-dressers, there are few psychological revelations. Indeed, how could there be at a time when transvestism was not considered to be a distinct or separate condition? Both Mary Frith and Charlotte Charke simply enumerate the events and details of their lives, treating their cross-dressing as a malign trick of fate. If they consider it at all, it is only to confirm received opinion – as though it were an external and invasive force, rather than a specific or subjective orientation. Although the Abbé de Choisy is not so objective, and therefore moralistic, about his condition, his memoirs are marked

141

The frontispiece to an 1898 series of six drawings illustrating Théophile Gautier's Mademoiselle de Maupin

by self-analysis of only the lightest kind. Indeed, transvestism itself encourages a flattening and deadening of style. De Choisy's narcissism and auto-eroticism are such, for example, that his prose does not connect in any way with a substantial or recognizable reality. His style is fanciful, his tone coquettish and, although the detailed enumeration of his female costumes suggests the working of fetishistic elements, the deliberately gay and superficial nature of his memoirs bears all the marks of a repressive mechanism erasing the actual content of his obsessions.

His own imaginative study of cross-dressing, *The Story of the Marquise–Marquis de Banneville*, is no less whimsical. The narrative recounts the history of a boy, known as 'La belle Marianne', who has been dressed as a girl from earliest infancy and has no idea of his real sex. Clamped in iron bodices, he grows into a model young lady: '"After giving the whole of the morning to my mind," she would say in her agreeable way, "it is only fair to give the afternoon to my eyes, my mouth and to my entire little person."' Marianne eventually falls in love with a handsome young man, dressed in the effeminate style of the period: 'he had dazzling diamond rings in his ears, and three or four patches on his face'. They make gentle love and soon marry, but the potentially explosive nature of such a relationship is defused when the young man turns out to have been, all the time, a girl in masquerade. The implication of this fable is that transvestism can be a socially acceptable and ultimately safe activity; the narrative acts as a parody of conventional love literature, and one of the most interesting and imaginative uses of transvestism is as a form of anti-romance in which normally unmentionable feelings (the hint of lesbianism in the mother's relationship to the cross-dressed son, the overt homosexuality in Marianne's attraction to young men) can be ambiguously set forth without causing offence. It can become a kind of pastoral – as in Shakespeare, for example – where normally repressed fantasies are illuminated and enjoyed.

It is really only in the prose literature of the nineteenth and twentieth centuries that cross-dressing, with all the sexual ambiguity which it implies, takes on an imaginative and symbolic life. Gautier's *Mademoiselle de Maupin* (1835) came as something of a revelation in this respect. The novel takes its name from the seventeenth-century actress who dressed as a man in order to seduce women, and from this unpromising material Gautier has constructed a plot of some subtlety and resonance. The narrative opens ambiguously enough when the narrator, a poet called D'Albert, begins to question his own sexual identity: '. . . they alleged that my clothes were too girlish in style. My hair, they further remarked, was too elaborately curled . . .'.

When D'Albert first encounters Mademoiselle de Maupin, who is dressed as a man under the name of Théodore, he is immediately perturbed: 'He carries himself with perfect grace.' And when he falls in love with 'Théodore', he is invaded by powers that he hardly understands: 'Already I have one foot poised in the empty air and feel that, before very long, the other one will follow it. I am convinced that all resistance on my part is useless, and that I am fated to be hurled into the depths of this new abyss which is beginning to yawn within me. . . . I love a man.'

This terror, evoked by 'Théodore's' cross-dressing, causes D'Albert to doubt his own sexual and social nature: 'I no longer feel certain who I am or what others are, I am left wondering whether I am a man or woman.' Cross-dressing has, in an unacknowledged way, broken down the sexual code and changed the nature of D'Albert's perceptions: 'I feel as utterly isolated as anyone can be, and all the links between myself and external objects, and between external objects and myself, have been broken one by one.' This is a clear statement of the disorientation which cross-dressing can induce, but in the process 'I comprehend many, many things which I never used to comprehend, I perceive amazing affinities for the first time.' Although the notion of homosexuality is primarily responsible for the abasement and renewal of

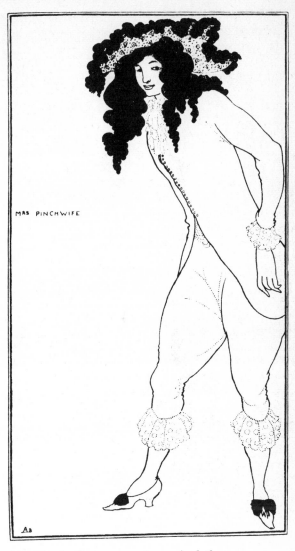

Mrs Pinchwife, a woman in man's clothes. Engraving by Beardsley

Vita Sackville-West dressed as Orlando

D'Albert's spirit, the experience itself is deeply implicated in Gautier's presentation of transvestism; and the novel becomes a meditation on the artistic and sexual nature of camouflage, and the role of metaphorical concealment.

Mademoiselle de Maupin herself at first adopts the conventional attitude towards her cross-dressing: 'madcap as I am . . .', she remarks, echoing the 'roaring girl' sentiments of stage heroines. But her transvestism goes further than any harmless 'breeches' part: 'I possess hardly a womanly attribute except a bosom . . . It is my body but not my mind which wears a skirt. Beneath my smooth forehead and silky tresses, male and ruthless thoughts are astir.' It is as if de Maupin herself were here evoking the image of the phallic woman which characteristically informs the fantasies of male transvestites. Certainly the split between her sex and her gender is clear enough, a division which has the capacity to destroy the sexist cycle of submission and domination: 'I am free from women's foolish servility, diffidence and petty-mindedness; I am free from men's wicked ways, gross lechery and brutish tastes. I belong to a third sex of its own which has not yet been given a name; higher or lower, better or worse . . . My imaginary ideal would have to be of each sex in turn.' Eventually, the lady vanishes. *Mademoiselle de Maupin* is an extraordinary novel of transvestitic fantasy, culminating in sexual reversals of the most radical kind.

This idea of the 'third sex' is a peculiarly nineteenth-century notion; androgynous images infuse the art and the literature of the period, and such images are inevitably although indirectly linked to transvestism. In Balzac's *Seraphita* (1836), for example, the ambiguous being after whom the book is named resembles both in nature and in spirit the transvestitic shamans of earlier times. Seraphitus is introduced as 'the being' whose manner 'bespoke a certain negation'. His sex changes continually and he wears 'a formless garment which resembles equally a woman's robe and a man's mantle'. He/she says, evoking the alienated role of the primitive shaman, 'I am an exile, far from heaven; a monster, far from earth.' And the bisexuality or androgyny involved is explicitly connected with certain holy powers: '. . . her thought is an intelligent sight which enables her to perceive all things in their essence, and to connect them with the general evolution of the Universe'. Essential 'sight', in other words, is available only after the inversion and destruction of ordinary sexual roles.

Virginia Woolf's fictional biography *Orlando* creates a similarly spiritual and timeless being – Orlando changes from male to female after a supernatural visitation in Turkey, like some comic variant on the shamanistic trance – but his powers are more directly linked with the changing of his clothes: 'There is much to support the view that it is clothes that wear us, and not we them; we may make them take the mould of arm or breast, but they mould our hearts, our brains, our tongues to their liking . . . it is often only the clothes that keep the male or female likeness, while underneath the sex is the very opposite of what it is above.' By being able to experience both sexes, in one irreversible act of cross-dressing, Orlando is able to live as an eternal being.

Cross-dressing is considered just as ironically and playfully – but with similar connotations – in Rhoides's *Pope Joan* (1886). This anti-clerical satire does not stray much from the apocryphal history of the female Pope but, within the farce of her sacred transvestism, there are hints of older and more primitive beliefs. She comes to Rome under the name of John and 'on the very day of Joanna's arrival in the city some sort of ceremony was being enacted in the churches in honour of the ancient gods'. On her election as Pope John, there was 'a heavy fall of snow, a rain of blood . . . a hail of dead locusts'. These numinous items are designed to complete the ecclesiastical parody, but Pope Joan clearly becomes a fearful figure in the process, a female transvestite who can alter the course of nature through her cross-dressing.

Transvestism has often become a rhetorical device in literature to symbolize anarchy

An illustration of the mythical pontiff from E.D. Rhoides's Pope Joan

Brian Deacon in the film version of The Triple Echo *(1972)*

of this, and other kinds. Once it has been presented, it tends to unbalance naturalistic conventions and the narratives which contain it often veer into confused surrealism or intimations of violence and disorder. In Sherwood Anderson's short story 'The Man Who Became A Woman', the transvestitic and trans-sexual images destroy its coherence and it turns into a muddled but murderous fable. In James Farrell's short story about transvestism, 'Just Boys' ('Princess Amy was wearing a trailing green formal dress and artificial breasts'), a party ends in inexplicable disaster. In H.E. Bates's *The Triple Echo*, the story of an army deserter who dresses as a woman in order to escape detection, the whole process of cross-dressing leads ineluctably to discovery and death.

Anthony Powell's more sophisticated account of male transvestism, in *From A View To A Death* (1939), is no less fearful. The central character here is Major Fosdick, a heterosexual transvestite who is first described as having 'the air of a legendary creature of the woods'. His life seems ordinary enough but, 'during a period of mental relaxation', Major Fosdick takes out a black sequin dress and a 'large picture hat': 'Removing his coat and waistcoat, Major Fosdick slipped the dress over his head and, shaking it so that it fell into position, he went to the looking glass and put on the hat. When he had arranged it at an angle that was to his satisfaction, he lit his pipe and, taking a copy of *Through The Western Highlands With Rod and Gun* from the dressing table, he sat down . . . For a good many years he had found it restful to do this for an hour or two every day when he had the opportunity . . .'. This unemotive description of cross-dressing has an air of cool neutrality, but one which is soon dispersed as the theme of 'dressing up' pervades and finally unbalances the novel. As always, it propels this conventionally realistic narrative into farce and melodrama as a way of dealing with otherwise explosive material. Major Fosdick is caught while dressed, and goes colourfully mad – 'Jabbering something awful, he was' – and the book ends with a number of deaths and disasters. In all of these imaginative accounts, transvestism is seen as a bizarre and threatening thing – an image which becomes so potent and pervasive that the narrative itself becomes a victim of its anarchy and disassociation.

Only in the context of fantasy, of allegory, or even of sheer playful inventiveness, does cross-dressing take on more substantial life. In overtly homosexual novels, for example, transvestism is handled sensationally but with less difficulty. John Rechy's portrait of homosexual transvestites in *City of Night* skilfully evokes that world which floats somewhere between drag and fetishism: 'queens can do it better than most real girls, queens being Uninhibited'. There is a sexual and social defiance, a theatrical aggressiveness, which Rechy captures very well: 'But one day, in the most lavish drag you've evuh seen – heels! and gown! and beads! and spangled earrings! – I'm going to storm heaven and protest! Here I am!!!! I'll yell – and I'll shake my beads at Him . . . and God will cringe!!'

God will turn away from this entirely self-made creature, an amalgam of both sexes, who owes his origin to no force in heaven or earth. There is a kind of reckless defiance of all natural laws at the centre of homosexual and heterosexual transvestism, and it is one which invokes images of chaos and instability. At the Mardi Gras pageant in New Orleans, Rechy writes: 'an almost Biblical feeling of Doom – of the city about to be destroyed, razed, toppled – assaults you'. The dark side of transvestism emerges steadily throughout *City of Night* in emblems of pain and loneliness; in one scene, a transvestite is ridiculed by a married couple: 'And I will think later that in that moment she must have felt the paint like pain on her face . . . her whole massive body seemed to be struggling against something – perhaps that absurd fate – against the shackles of that dress, those rings, beads, sequins . . . *himself*! – crushed by that something too overwhelmingly unfair to define.'

Genet explores another aspect of homosexual transvestism in *The Thief's Journal*; it is an account of the Carolinas of Barcelona, the transvestitic prostitutes who wait for clients at the pissoirs. And Genet, like Rechy, emphasises the chaos and despair at the heart of their activity: 'But remote in these limbos, they cause curious disasters which are harbingers of new beauties. One of them, Theresa the Great . . . would bring a camp chair to one of the circular urinals near the harbour and would sit down inside and do her knitting or crocheting. She would stop to eat a sandwich. She was at home . . . Senorita Dora was another. Dora would exclaim in a shrill voice, "What bitches they are, those awful she-men!" From the memory of this cry is born a brief but profound meditation on their despair, which was mine.'

Homosexual transvestism, of this and other kinds, has always been an available theme for the novelist, both because of its readily identifiable characteristics and its accessibility as a social phenomenon. Heterosexual transvestism has never afforded the same imaginative or social access; indeed, the only accurate presentation emerges in Geoff Brown's novel, *I Want What I Want* (1966). It is both a sympathetic and an objective account, and the clarity of the writing distinguishes it from the coy and secretive accounts generally to be obtained from male transvestites themselves.

Roy Clark, an ordinary and rather nondescript boy, is convinced that he is a woman – with the refrain, 'I want what I want, not what I ought to want.' He experiments with cross-dressing, and is promptly confined to a mental hospital to be relieved of his curious pleasures. Here transvestism is presented in its more ferocious aspect, at the hospital's annual dance where some of the male patients cross-dress: 'I thought of a savage islander of the Pacific who had killed and eaten a lady missionary and then put on her clothes.' The mixture of exhibitionism, desire and aggression evoked here is extraordinarily acute, and the condition of the transvestite is placed in an even sharper focus when Roy Clark himself dresses up: 'I might have shouted, "This is what we have become! Once only our stomach and our sex had desire, but now our brain has desire! Madness is the lust of the brain!"'

It is precisely this 'lust of the brain' which Roy reveals on his discharge, when he cross-dresses and transforms himself into 'Wendy Ross': 'I was dressing up. Everything was better than it had been.' There are some closely rendered descriptions of the loneliness and secrecy involved in this activity, and there are also suggestions of the violence and masochistic anger that can be associated with transvestism: 'When the sadist tortured the bound woman his cruelty was his anger

that he was not the woman.' But dressing up also provides a kind of liberation: 'I was selfish and I was establishing my personality. I was not living as a social unit. I was living consciously.' But this freedom is won at the expense of exclusion from the ordinary social community. And it may be that the narcissism of the transvestite is in part a defence against the fears and anxieties which such an exclusion may induce.

Roy/Wendy is clearly not at ease with his own cross-dressing: 'I was glad that I was suffering. It was a woman's suffering. I was a bitch . . . it was right that I should be stopped and frustrated. I was female.' And, at the end of the book, Roy/Wendy takes pills and tries to 'commit suicide while of unsound sex'. It is a depressing, and in some ways depressingly predictable, conclusion. But *I Want What I Want* bears the same marks which transvestites themselves have to carry, and the novel is so powerfully written that it is one of the most extraordinary contemporary documents of transvestism.

It is certainly more coherent and substantial than most of the transvestitic literature which is written by and for transvestites and trans-sexuals. In some instances the transvestitic fetish is so pervasive that the writing breaks under the strain. The short stories and the novellas are, for example, often dominated by tactile sensations and intimations of texture: 'He had the sensation that his legs were prisoners of the wispy black nylon'; or the transvestite joyfully suffers confinement in female clothes: 'As he moved to the bed the tightness of the girdle gave him a feeling of constriction that somehow harmonised in his mind with the role he was assuming.'

Often the transvestite is punished for his obsession by an Amazonian creature: 'You remember I asked you not to wear a corset tonight so I could really whip your bottom properly.' And on other occasions the transvestite will identify himself with the phallic woman: '. . . when I don my platinum wig and

(Opposite) *Two drag queens at the New Orleans Mardi Gras*

148

attire myself in frilly, female undies, black nylons, high heels, long black cotton gloves, beautiful jewellery and tight-fitting toreador pants, I feel like a living Goddess who expects to be loved and worshipped and obeyed'. The banality and repetitiveness of this pornography testify to the depth of the obsessions which are being enacted, and the dominant image might be said to be that of the omnipotent mother who is both desirable and distressing. Gillian Freeman has remarked, in *The Undergrowth of Literature*, how similar images occur in children's comics – 'Wonder Woman', for example, has steel bracelets and a gold, whip-like lasso and is 'the essence of aggressive womanhood'; this reinforces the analytical belief in the essentially infantile nature of the transvestitic obsession. Equally, it might be said that the phallic woman reinstates the image of the bisexual deities worshipped by the transvestitic shamans. However we interpret it, that image persists and is deeply implicated in the rituals of cross-dressing.

Indeed, when it is absent, the writings of transvestites tend to become secretive and skittish. The real nature of the obsession is camouflaged in apparent aspirations toward a kind of giggly girlishness. This division, between the decorous and 'lady-like' surface of the transvestite and the fetishism which exists beneath, is a large one but it has been forced upon transvestites by the culture itself. At the same time as they become attached to the sexual stereotypes of femininity, they internalize all the guilt publicly attached to their condition and thus the fetish grows. The division works on every level – but, in the context of the written word, it manifests itself in the transition from coy and ornate prose to the excessive vulgarity of transvestitic pornography.

Since the condition is essentially auto-erotic, the visual pornography seems peculiarly rootless and inhumane. Transvestitic models adopt obscene poses, but always alone, their genitals visible beneath the female underwear in a parody of secrecy and lust. But the images lack resonance and definition; they are much flatter and cruder than most homosexual or heterosexual pornography, principally because the context of, and audience for, the obsession is so ill-defined. The accompanying captions imitate the insubstantiality of these images by using the language of vulgar femininity – 'GIRL, a person's got to sleep sometime don't they?' – without having any of its vitality. This is perhaps why the analytical explanation of the sexual roots of transvestism is not entirely convincing: when transvestism is treated as a sexual phenomenon, it becomes overblown and lifeless, borrowing its vocabulary and images from elsewhere. If it were necessary to prove that transvestism is not primarily or exclusively a sexual activity, its pornography would be a good witness.

(Opposite) *Anne Heywood in a scene from* I Want What I Want *(1971), adapted from the novel by Geoff Brown*

BIBLIOGRAPHY

ATKINS J.A. *Sex in Literature* London, 1970

BABCOCK Barbara A. (ed.) *The Reversible World. Symbolic Inversion in Art and Society.* New York, 1978

BAKER Roger *Drag. A History of Female Impersonation on the Stage* London, 1968

BENEDICT Ruth *Patterns of Culture* New York, 1935

BENJAMIN Harry *The Transsexual Phenomenon* New York, 1966

BLOCH Ivan *Sexual Life in England Past and Present* London, 1938

CADÉAC M. *Le Chevalier d'Eon et son problème psycho-sexuel* Paris, 1966

CAULDWELL David (ed.) *Transvestism* New York, 1956

COSTA Mario *Reverse Sex. The Life of Jacqueline Charlotte Dufresnoy* London, 1961

COX Cynthia *The Enigma of the Age. The Strange Story of the Chevalier D'Eon* London, 1966

CRAWLEY Ernest *Dress, Drink and Drums* London, 1931

—— *The Mystic Rose. A Study of Primitive Marriage* London, 1902

CROFT-COOKE Rupert *Feasting With Panthers* London, 1967

DELCOURT Marie *Hermaphrodite* Paris, 1958

ELIADE Mircea *Le Chamanisme et les techniques archaïques de l'extase* Paris, 1951

—— *Naissances mystiques* Paris, 1959

ELLIS Henry Havelock *Studies in the Psychology of Sex* Philadelphia, 1910

FLUGEL J.C. *The Psychology of Clothes* London, 1930

FREEMAN Gillian *The Undergrowth of Literature* London, 1967

FREUD Sigmund *Drei Abhandlungen zur Sexualtheorie* Teschen 1905 (trans. James Strachey, London 1962)

GILBERT O.P. *Men in Women's Guise* London, 1926

—— *Women in Men's Guise* London, 1932

HERIOT Angus *The Castrati in Opera* London, 1956

HIRSCHFELD Magnus *Sexual Anomalies and Perversions* London, 1946

KAY Barry *The Other Women* London, 1976

LANGNER Lawrence *The Importance of Wearing Clothes* London, 1960

MANDER Raymond and MITCHENSON Joe *British Music Hall: a Story in Pictures* London, 1965

—— *Musical Comedy: a Story in Pictures* London, 1969

MARMOR Judd (ed.) *Sexual Inversion. The Multiple Roots of Homosexuality* New York, 1965

NIXON Edna *Royal Spy. The Strange Case of the Chevalier d'Eon* New York, 1965

OVERZIER Claus (ed.) *Intersexuality* Stuttgart, 1961

PRONKO Leonard *Theater East and West* Berkeley and Los Angeles, 1967

SAVICH Evgeny *Homosexuality, Transvestism and Change of Sex* London, 1958

STOLLER Robert *Sex and Gender* New York, 1968

STORR Anthony *Sexual Deviation* London, 1964

TABORI Paul *Dress and Undress. The Sexology of Fashion* London, 1969

TAYLOR Gordon Rattray *Sex in History* London, 1953

THOMPSON C.J.S. *Mysteries of Sex* London, 1938

TYLER Parker *Screening the Sexes. Homosexuality in the Movies* New York, 1972

SOURCES OF ILLUSTRATIONS

INDEX

Page references in *italic* type indicate illustrations

Achilles 46
actresses 95–6
Adam 39
Africa, African peoples 37, *39*, 40, 42, 43, 46, *47*
Albania *43*
Alcuin 52
Alembert, Jean d' 10
anarchy, transvestism and 51–2, 54, 145–6, 147
Anderson, Frances 86
Anderson, Sherwood 147
androgyny, *see* hermaphroditism
Aphrodite, Bearded 39
Arabs 43
Arbuckle, Fatty 122
Archenholz, Johann Wilhelm von 58, 98
Ariadne 39
Aristophanes 48
Artemis 40, 46
Ashton, Frederick *103*
Asterius, St 52
Astrée, L' (d'Urfé) 141
Australia *18*, *19*, *22*, 24
Aztecs 37, 40

Bachaumont, Louis Petit de 78
Baker, Roger 104–7
ballet 118
Ballets Trokadero de Monte Carlo, Les *116–17*, 118
Balzac, Honoré de 144–5
Bancroft, John 31
Bannister, Charles 99
Barbette *106*
Bard, Wilkie 101
'Barker, Colonel' *86*
'Barrie, Barbara' 23
'Barry, James' 82, *82*
Bates, H.E. 146–7
Baxter, Stanley *136*
Beardsley, Aubrey *140*, *143*
Beaujolais 54
Beaumarchais, Pierre-Augustin Caron de 78
Beaumont Society 23
Beckford, William 98
Beerbohm, Max 101

Beggar's Opera, The 98, *99*
Benedict, Ruth 37
berdaches 36, 37
Berlin 64
Bernhardt, Sarah 93
Bhoota dancers *49*
bisexuality, *see* hermaphroditism
Bloch, Ivan 60
Bonny, Ann 76, *76*
Borneo 40
Boulton, Edward, and Frederick Park *83*, 83–5
Bowie, David 120, *121*
boy actors, child actors 57, 90–92
Brazil 37, *38*, 39, 43
breeches parts 96, 101
Brown, Geoff 148, *150*
Brown, Wally *131*
Bruegel, Pieter *55*
Buddhism 95

Cadéac, M. 81
Caligula 69
Carney, Alan *131*
carnival 54, *55*, *58*
castrati 98
castration 29, 30
Celebes 42
Ceylon *48*, *49*
Chaos 37, 48, 52
Chaplin, Charlie 122, *124*
Charke, Charlotte 76–7, 141
Charles Edward Stuart ('Bonnie Prince Charlie') *85*
child actors, boy actors 57, 90–92
China 57, 94–5
Choisy, Abbé de 9–10, *73*, 73–4, 141–2
Christianity, medieval 52
Christina, Queen, of Sweden 69–70
Chukchee 40
cinema 122–30
circumcision 46, 52
City of Night (Rechy) 147
clothes, dress 34, 74
clubs, homosexual 58–64
Coccinelle 107, *107*
Colette *87*
Cooper, Alice 120

Cooper, Fenimore 141
Cotys 48
Crawford, Joan *132*
Crawley, Ernest 43
Creation myths 37
Cycle Sluts, the *50*
Cyprus 39

Dahomey *39*
Darling, Candy 114
Davenant, Sir William 95
Davies, Christina *74*, 74–5
Davis, Natalie 72
Deacon, Brian *146*
Delcourt, Marie 71
Dessy-Dreyfus, Claude 114–18
Dietrich, Marlene 122, *127*
Dijon 54
Dionysos 46, 52, 89
disguise or concealment, in literature 141
Dortmund 66
drag 13–14, 104–14, 122–30
drama, *see* theatre
dress, *see* clothes
Dyaks 40

Edinburgh 54
Edward, Prince (later Edward VIII) *28*
Eliade, Mircea 48
Ellis, Henry Havelock 27, 77
Eltinge, Julian *12, 20, 21, 28, 29*, 112, *112*
Emery, Dick *137*
Emil August, Duke 70–71
Eno, Brian *120*
Eon, Chevalier d' 77–82, *79, 80, 81*
Ephesus 40
Ernst-Strauss, Louise *134*
Eskimos 40
Esquirol, Jean 25

Farrell, James 147
fertility, vegetation 39, 46–8, 89, 94–5
fetishism 14, 20, 25, 73–4, 151
Fielding, Henry 76
Flake, Otto *134*
Fletcher, Cyril 102
Fools, Feast of 52, 52–3
Frazer, James 40, 46
Freeman, Gillian 151

Freud, Sigmund 27, 28, 29
Frith, Mary *68*, 72, 141
From A View To A Death (Powell) 147

Garbo, Greta 122
Gasperone Group, the *113*
Gautier, Théophile *142*, 143–4
Genet, Jean 147–9
Ginkeyn, El- 57
Goethe, Johann Wolfgang von 54, 98
Golden Rule Pleasure Club 64
Grande Eugène, La 114–19
Greece, ancient *40*, 46–8, *52*, 89, *90*
Greek Anthology, The 141
Grimaldi, Joseph 98
Guinness, Alec 122, *123*

Hall, Radclyffe *86*
Hamilton, Molly 76
harvest festivals 39, 46–8
Hat-Shepsūt, Queen *46*
Haxells Hotel 61
Hearne, Richard *104*
Heliogabalus 69
Helpmann, Robert *103*
Henry III, of France 70
Hensey, Florence *85*
Hera 46
Hercules 42
hermaphroditism, androgyny, bisexuality 25–7, 37–9, *40, 41*, 144–5
Herodotus 40, 51–2
Heywood, Anne *150*
Hinge and Bracket *138*
Hirschfeld, Magnus 27, 28, 30–31, 64, 66, 70
Hitchcock, Alfred 130
Hitler, Adolf 34
Holloway, Robert, 60–61
homosexuality 14, 23–4, 25, 57, 58–60, 77, 83
  in literature 141, 147–9
Hope, Bob 122, *122*
House, Billy *130*
Humphries, Barry *139*
Hybristika 46
Hyde, Edward *84*, 85–6

I Want What I Want (Brown) 148, *150*
Incas 37, 40
India 40, *42, 49*, 57
Indians, North American *36*, 37, 40, 57

infancy, infantile experiences 21, 27–9, 30, 73, 138
Innocent XI, Pope 9
Inslip Club 61
Ishtar 57
Isidore of Seville 52

Jacobus X 64
Jagger, Mick 120, 130
Japan 24
  male geishas in 57
  theatre in *88*, 89, *94*, 94–5
Jefferini 98–101
Joan of Arc, 71, *71*
Juvenal 141

Kabuki theatre *88*, 95
Kalends 51–2
Kathakali dancers *48*, *49*
Kay, Barry 24
Keaton, Buster 122, *127*
Kemp, Lindsay *108*
Krafft-Ebing, Richard von 25
Kyd, Thomas *91*
Kynaston, Edward 96, *96*

La Rue, Danny 107, *110*
Lacan, Jacques 30
Lacretelle, Jean de 82
Lambert, Joe 86
Leno, Dan *101*, 101–3
Lévi-Strauss, Claude 95
Lewis, Ioan 40
Lewis, Jerry *128–9*
Lisa-Maron 37–8
literature (*see also* theatre), transvestism in 141–51
Logan, Andrew *109*
London, homosexual clubs in 58–64
Luddite riots 54
Lüthi, Urs 118–19, *119*

Macrobius 39
Mademoiselle de Maupin 142, 143–4
Mard Brothers 98
Mardi Gras *11*, *32–3*, *51*, *149*
marriage *12*, 23
Marshall, E.W. 101
Martial 141

Marx, Groucho 122
Masai 46
Maximus the Confessor 39
Mayas 40
mental illness, transvestism as 25, 27, 31
Mere Folle 54
Middle Ages 52, 71, 90
Mills, Ann *77*
Misrule, Abbeys of 54
Misrule, Lord of 52
'Monsieur' (Duc d'Orléans) 9, *69*, 70
Moriss, Violette *13*
Morris, Jan 37
mothers, mother-fixation 23, 27–9, 30
Motteville, Mlle de 70
mummers *53*, 90
Munday, Anthony 54
music hall 101

Naogeorgus 52
Napheys, Dr 64
New Orleans *11*, *32–3*, *51*, *149*
New York 64, *113*
New York Dolls 114, *115*
Nixon, Edna 78, 81
Noh drama *94*, 94–5, 95
Norman, Karyl *66*, 112

Olivier, Laurence *92*, *122*
onnagata 89, 95
opera, castrati in 98
Orlando (Woolf) 145
Oschophoria 46

pantomime 98–104
Paris
  medieval 52
  19th century 57, 64
  20th century *62–3*, *106*
Parkhurst (clergyman) 64
Pelagia, St 71
Pelew Islands 40
penis 28–9
Pepys, Samuel 96
performance, *see* theatre
'phallic woman' 28–9, 30, 148–51
Picabia, Francis *134*
Picasso, Pablo *135*
Pickford, Mary *130*
Pierce, Charles 114

Polanski, Roman *133*
politics, political dissent, transvestism and 10, 54
Pope Joan 71
Pope Joan (Rhoides) 145, *145*
pornography, transvestitic 24, 30, 148–51
Porteous riots 54
Powell, Anthony 147
Powell, William *127*
primitive peoples, transvestism among 27, 37–48
 passim
Pronko, Leonard 95
prostitution, transvestitic/homosexual *18*, 54–7,
 56, 141, 147–8
Prynne, William 92–4
pseudo-Byron 141
psychologists, transvestism studied by 24–31
Punch 34, *34*
punk 74
Puritans, theatres closed by 94, 95

Rajshahi *42*
Read, Mary 76, *76*
'Rebecca' 54
Rechy, John 147
religion, sacred rituals, transvestism in 10, 37–48
Renault, Francis 112
Rhoides, Emmanuel D. 145, *145*
Ridiculous, Theatre of the 114
rites of passage 46
Roberts, Pudgy *111*
Robey, George *100*, 101
rock culture *115*, 120–22
Roeg, Nicholas *118*
Rome
 ancient 39, 42, 69, *89*, 89–90, *91*, 141
 modern 54
Rooney, Mickey 122, *124*
Rose, June 82
Rowlandson, Tom 86

Sackville-West, Vita *144*
sado-masochism 30, 148
Salisbury Hob Nob *53*
Sand, George *85*
Sardanapalus *70*
Satan's Harvest Home 58
Saturnalia 51–2
'Saul, Jack' 61–4
Savalette de Lange, Jenny de 86
Savoy and Brennan 112–14
schizophrenia 27, 31

Scott, Malcolm 101
Scythians 40, 52
Seraphita (Balzac) 144–5
sexual deviation, transvestism as 10; *see also*
 mental illness
sexual excitement, transvestism and 14, 21, 27–8,
 30–31; *see also* pornography
Shakespeare, William 92, 142
shamanism 37–48 *passim*
Shango 38, *38*
Shrovetide 52, 54
Silentarius, Paulus 141
Singapore *56*
'Skimmington, Lady' 54
Smith, Jack 130
Snell, Hannah *74*, 75
society, social order, transvestism as attack on 10,
 54, 64
Some Like It Hot 122, *125*
Spy, The (Cooper) 141
Stockport 54
Stoller, Robert 29–30, 122
Stubbes, Philip 52
Swor, Bert 112
Sydney, Australia *16–17*, *18*, *19*

Tahiti 37
Talbot, Mary Anne ('James Taylor') 75, *75*
Tassaert *8*
'Taylor, James' (Mary Anne Talbot) 75, *75*
theatre 9, 57, 75, 76, 89–138
Thief's Journal, The (Genet) 147
Thomas, Augustine *134*
Tilley, Vesta 101
trans-sexuals, trans-sexualism 13–14, *14*, 25, 29, 77,
 107
transvestism 10–24
 causes of, theories concerning 10, 24–34, 151
 female 30, 71–2, 74–7, 82–3
 and fetishism, *see* fetishism
 first use of the term 27
 and homosexuality, *see* homosexuality
 incidence of 14
transvestites, anxiety, etc. suffered by 18, 20, 21–2,
 72
Troubridge, Una Lady 86
Twiggy *110*
Tyler, Parker 122

Ugly Sisters, the 101, 102–4, *103*
'unisex' 74
Urfé, Honoré d' 141

Vacarro, John 114
Vallabha sect 40
vegetation, deities/rites concerning, *see* fertility
Vere Street coterie 60–61
Vestris, Madame 102, *102*
Vienna 64
Visconti, Luchino *126*, 130

Westermarck, Edward Alexander 37
Westphal, Carl 25
Whiteboys 54
'Wildfire, Madge' 54
William, Prince (later Duke of Gloucester) *26*
Wilson, A. E. 102
Wilson, Edmund 114
Wiltshire, peasant riots in 54

women
    male transvestites' attitudes to 14, 23, 107–12
    see also actresses; mothers; 'phallic woman';
    transvestism, female
Woodlawn, Holly 114, *114*
Woolf, Virginia 145
Wyndham, Francis 114–18

Yakut 42
Yansan 39, 43

Zoli, W. *13*
Zoyara, Ella 86
Zulus 43
zunkhas 57